CLOSING THE ATTITUDE GAP

How to Fire Up Your Students to Strive for Success

CLOSING THE ATTITUDE GAP

How to Fire Up Your Students to Strive for Success

BARUTI K.
KAFELE

CLOSING THE
ATTITUDE GAP

How to Fire Up Your Students to Strive for Success

Alexandria, Virginia USA

ASCD®

1703 N. Beauregard St. • Alexandria, VA 22311-1714 USA
Phone: 800-933-2723 or 703-578-9600 • Fax: 703-575-5400
Website: www.ascd.org • E-mail: member@ascd.org
Author guidelines: www.ascd.org/write

Gene R. Carter, *Executive Director;* Mary Catherine (MC) Desrosiers, *Chief Program Development Officer;* Richard Papale, *Publisher;* Genny Ostertag, *Acquisitions Editor;* Julie Houtz, *Director, Book Editing & Production;* Ernesto Yermoli, *Editor;* Lindsey Smith, *Graphic Designer;* Mike Kalyan, *Production Manager;* Valerie Younkin, *Desktop Publishing Specialist*

Printed in the United States of America. Cover art © 2013 by ASCD. ASCD publications present a variety of viewpoints. The views expressed or implied in this book should not be interpreted as official positions of the Association.

PAPERBACK ISBN: 978-1-4166-1628-3   ASCD product #114006   n8/13

Also available as an e-book (see Books in Print for the ISBNs).

Quantity discounts: 10–49 copies, 10%; 50+ copies, 15%; for 1,000 or more copies, call 800-933-2723, ext. 5634, or 703-575-5634. For desk copies: www.ascd.org/deskcopy.

Library of Congress Cataloging-in-Publication Data
Kafele, Baruti K.
    Closing the attitude gap: how to fire up your students to strive for success / Baruti K. Kafele
        pages cm
    Includes bibliographical references and index.
    ISBN 978-1-4166-1628-3 (pbk. : alk. paper)   1. Motivation in education.
2. Academic achievement.   3. Teacher-student relationships.   4. Teachers—Attitudes.   5. Students—Attitudes.   I. Title.
    LB1065.K257 2013
370.15'4—dc23
2013019637

23 22 21 20 19 18 17 16 15 14   2 3 4 5 6 7 8 9 10 11 12

*This book is dedicated to all of the students and staff
I have had the privilege of working with throughout
my 24 years as a classroom teacher, building
principal, and educational consultant.*

*As the African proverb states: I am,
because we are—and because we are, I am.*

INTRODUCTION

In August of 2009, ASCD published my book, *Motivating Black Males to Achieve in School and in Life*. From the moment that book hit the market, my life changed dramatically. Prior to writing it, I was the principal of Newark Tech High School in Newark, New Jersey. As I say to everyone, I was born for this work; throughout my 14 years as an urban public school principal, it was my heartfelt conviction that I was living my *passion*. I absolutely loved waking up in the morning and going to Newark Tech to motivate, educate, and empower—to lead. In fact, I loved what I did so much that I stopped referring to myself as Baruti K. Kafele and began to refer to myself as "Principal Kafele," even when I was away from the school. I felt that in order for me to maximize my own potential as an educator and a principal, I had to be Principal Kafele 24/7. (It caught on: Now everyone calls me Principal Kafele.)

The student population at Newark Tech was about 70 percent black and 30 percent Latino. About 85 percent of students received free or reduced-priced lunch. The school had never met the benchmark for adequate yearly progress prior to my arrival. Partly as a result of my keen focus on transforming student attitudes, test scores began to soar after I arrived to such an extent that the school soon received national recognition.

As these great accomplishments were happening at Newark Tech, *Motivating Black Males to Achieve in School and in Life* was gaining momentum. My phone started ringing ceaselessly and the emails streamed in steadily. School and district administrators from all over the United States and abroad were calling on me to conduct workshops at their schools. They identified a desperate need for solutions toward motivating their black male students.

Over two solid years, demand continued to grow. I was torn as to what to do: stay at Newark Tech and live my passion as the building principal, or leave the school to meet this national and international demand? After wrestling with this decision for two years, I finally decided to meet the demand. What a difficult decision it was to leave the school that I had poured my heart and soul into for six years. Despite my passion for the work, I was an emotional wreck for the entire first year after I left Newark Tech. And yet, here I was, on July 1, 2011, starting on a new mission with the sole purpose of providing educators with strategies to motivate their black male learners.

Before moving forward, let me address my usage of the word *mission*. Never do I refer to what I do and what we as educators do as a job, profession, or career—not during these desperate times. I couldn't work at an optimal level if I did so. Instead, I refer to my work as a mission. When I think of a mission, I think of work that not only *must* be done, but *will* be done. I have to keep going and going and going until all students are successful, because their success as students is tied to my success as an educator. (You'll find more of my thoughts on education as a mission in Chapter 2.)

As I got out into the field as a full-time consultant, I met educators in city after city and town after town who were desperately seeking answers. No matter what part of the country I traveled, I met educators who were eager to learn more on meeting the needs of their black male learners.

At the core of my workshops on motivating black males is the idea of an *attitude gap*. I believe strongly that unless we focus on the attitudes of black males first and foremost, we are only spinning our wheels; the best math, reading, and writing strategies that money could buy aren't going to raise black male students' achievement alone. Far too many of us focus on closing the achievement gap without realizing that closing the attitude gap needs doing first. I am convinced that black males must have an "attitude of excellence" before actually experiencing excellence.

As I spread this message of attitude transformation across the country, it occurred to me that I should write a book on the importance of closing the attitude gap. A year after leaving Newark Tech, I checked into a New Jersey hotel with the intent of writing the foundation for this book without interruption. Because the concept of the attitude gap is not applicable only to black males, I decided to broaden the scope of this new book to address at-risk children of all racial and ethnic groups.

I took a week off my speaking engagements to start the project. My plan was to spend five days at the hotel and to write at least 5,000 words per day, so that by the time Friday evening arrived, I would have a solid foundation of 25,000 words to which I could then add over the next several weeks and months. Every day throughout the week, I focused my writing on the educators of at-risk urban children. At the end of each day, I would reluctantly surf the Internet for national news stories, just to stay in the know. I say "reluctantly" because I knew that the news would distract me from my writing, and distracted I became. One of the things that kept coming up in my searches was a significant increase in murders of black youth by other black youth, including innocent bystanders who were losing their lives to stray bullets while doing nothing more than playing outside on a hot summer day. Although these news stories troubled me to no end, they were nothing new to me. As I continued my work on the book and reflected upon the news stories of black-on-black violence, I began to feel that I ought to reverse course and focus my book more narrowly on black children.

After I checked out of the hotel, I immediately went back on the road, speaking to countless urban and rural school educators in daylong workshops. Only a few of these workshops addressed black children specifically; most addressed children of color in general. Educators at the workshops seemed truly inspired and told me that they felt ready to immediately implement the strategies I covered. These educators were starving for information that would further inspire their learners to develop the will to strive for excellence. It soon became clear to me that the message of my book needed to be expanded not only beyond solely black learners, but beyond solely urban learners as well.

When September arrived, I started leading motivational assemblies in schools. Most of these schools were diverse, and several had majority white student populations. As I spoke to these kids about their attitudes toward school and life, I noticed it wasn't only the black and Latino students who were inspired—the white students were equally affected. At the conclusion of my assemblies, white students were among the kids approaching me to talk about their personal challenges and situations or just to say thank you and to shake my hand. Teachers, counselors, and administrators pointed out to me emphatically that the problem of poor attitude and lack of motivation was pervasive and in no way confined to students of color. Given that my message of attitude transformation resonated with children of all racial and ethnic groups, I definitively concluded that my book would address educators of all at-risk children, urban and rural, regardless of race or ethnicity.

Throughout my first year on the road full time, I have had countless one-on-one conversations with teachers and administrators about the plight of children of color in urban and rural schools. Several of the educators I have spoken with have broken down and cried in the midst of our conversations. Others have done so during question-and-answer periods after my presentations. It is an emotional topic, and educators want to see their students come to school every day striving to maximize their potential. I remind educators that students have the capacity to perform; the question is, do they have the *will*? I tell educators to stop focusing solely on achievement, examine their students' attitudes, and consider ways to get them excited about learning and the prospects for their futures.

Often, when I am presenting at a conference, I will also attend sessions for my own professional growth and to remain current within the field. I attend a wide range of sessions, including ones in which I have little personal interest, just to know what's out there. Every time I sit in on these sessions, it occurs to me that in order for the teachers to effectively implement the strategies being discussed, their students have to be willing to receive them—that is, they need to have a receptive attitude. Attitude is everything; students have got to want what they are given.

The topic of closing the attitude gap typically generates a wealth of discussion with my audiences. Everyone has so much to share and so many questions to ask that I often leave the presentation wishing I could have covered even more. This book serves as an opportunity for me to cover a lot more ground and begin to address the hundreds of emailed questions that I receive from educators from all over the country.

Each chapter of the book begins with a reflective exercise. Daily reflection is absolutely crucial to the success of your students. It is imperative that at the beginning and end of each day you stop and reflect upon your mission, assessing what works and what adjustments might need to be made. Throughout the book, I make references to experiences I had in schools I taught in, led, or visited as a consultant; I also make references to my children, each of whom has had a significant effect on my focus as an educator. It is my hope that this book will serve as a good starting point for a much broader national conversation on closing the attitude gap.

The book is written as a motivational handbook for educators. I cannot tell you the number of principals who have said one or more of the following to me before a presentation:

- "I really need you to fire up my teachers."
- "I need you to get my teachers pumped up."
- "I need you to motivate my staff."
- "I need you to really shake my teachers up."
- "My teachers don't realize the power that they have—I need you to remind them."
- "Please don't pull any punches with my staff."
- "Light them up!"

My personal motto is "I'm on fire." I want to ensure that you, too, are on fire and remain on fire for your students throughout the entire school year as you take your mission of teaching to the next level.

I would be remiss if I didn't mention that I do not personally characterize myself as a scholar, intellectual, researcher, or career consultant. Each of these roles has its place toward improving education and student outcomes, but none represents who I am. I am a *practitioner*—one who has been on the front lines of urban education for 21 years as a classroom teacher and building principal, and one who will one day return to those front lines. I therefore write from the vantage point of one who has lived and breathed teaching.

1 | How Climate and Culture Shape Attitude

REFLECTIVE QUESTIONS

Before reading this chapter, look into a mirror and ask yourself the following questions:

1. What do my students see in my classroom?

2. What do my students hear in my classroom?

3. What do my students feel in my classroom?

4. What do my students experience in my classroom?

5. Do I provide a learning environment that fosters the proper attitude for my students' success?

Educators have been focusing on the question of how to close the achievement gap as measured by results on state standardized assessments for as long as I've been a teacher. National data over the years reveal that the gap doesn't seem to be going anywhere. As I visit schools and school districts nationally, I notice that folks feel good when even the slightest improvements are made.

In all my time as an urban public school teacher and principal, I have maintained that my students, who happened to be majority black, were brilliant and highly capable, with the ability to achieve anything they set their sights on achieving. This was the premise underlying my mission. The achievement gap consequently did not make sense to me—it seemed to place my students at a deficit before the first lesson. I knew that I couldn't inspire my students to strive to maximize their potential if they entered my classroom or school with a deficit mindset. They had to be in the pilot's seat, ready to soar.

I began to ask questions about the achievement gap. Why is it so? What are the differences? What is it that allows one group to outperform the other? Is it biological? Is it mental? Is it social? Is it cultural? Is it economic? Is it political? I wanted answers. I wanted to know why it was that this achievement gap existed and persisted. As I began to examine the answers to each of my questions, it became clear to me that there was another type of gap that wasn't getting the attention it deserved: the attitude gap. I define the attitude gap as *the gap between those students who have the will to strive for academic excellence and those who do not.* The key words in the definition are "will to strive." Students need to have this will in order to succeed. Their will is their attitude; they have to *want* success. The challenge for teachers is that "will" can't be taught—it has to be unleashed! One of the purposes of this book is to assist you with doing just that—helping your students to unleash their will to strive for academic excellence.

Throughout my years of teaching and leading, I have worked with students who had to go home to deplorable situations. Even the walk to and from school could be a challenge for many, often more so than any course they may encounter in school. Many of my students lived in challenging neighborhoods that could easily sap the drive out of anyone. Neighborhoods that are plagued by gangs, drugs, and violence can be both psychologically and emotionally draining. The challenges of living in such neighborhoods can drastically inhibit motivation and learning. I say to educators frequently that although we should feel for students who live in such neighborhoods, we cannot feel sorry for them. Feeling sorry for them is not going to help them out of their situation. Students do not need our sympathy. They need our inspiration and encouragement to change their realities for the better. We must therefore continue to hold them accountable for nothing less than excellence. By doing so, we will show them that despite their hardships they will soar high because we are their teachers and leaders. Excuses are unacceptable. There is an African proverb that states, "He who cannot dance will say the drum is bad." We cannot afford to blame the drum. We must look deeply within ourselves and ask, "What are we doing to change our students' attitudes so that every day that they walk into my classroom, they are fired up and ready to excel?"

Attitude is everything. Consider my own experience: I went from repeating my sophomore year in high school to graduating college *summa cum laude*. What was the difference between these two periods in my life? What about other successful people who struggled tremendously but turned it around dramatically and became success stories? What was the commonality that enabled them to achieve? I have concluded that it is a change in attitude.

How Climate and Culture Affect Student Learning

When I was a 6th grade classroom teacher, a colleague shared with me that she was going to attend a big literacy conference over the weekend, because she felt that teaching reading to her struggling students was one of her deficiencies. She was excited about the prospect of learning new teaching strategies and was particularly eager to hear one of the featured speakers.

On Monday morning, I went to see my colleague in her classroom about a half-hour before school began. She was *on fire*! She told me that she could barely sleep because of all of the new strategies she'd learned at the conference that she wanted to implement immediately with her students, many of whom were at risk of failing.

After the first period, I returned to my colleague's classroom to see how the implementation of her newly acquired strategies went. When I arrived, she was sitting at her desk looking rather bewildered. I asked her what happened. She said that implementation was unsuccessful because of the behavior of her students. She shared with me that she spent more of the period disciplining her students than she spent teaching them. This did not surprise me at all. I honestly did not anticipate that the rollout of these new reading strategies would succeed because she had extreme climate and culture problems in her classroom. Despite her excitement, I knew that these problems would wind up eating the new strategies for breakfast! Clearly, the attitudes of my colleague's students prevented them from receiving the new strategies.

In classrooms across the United States, teachers are feeling the pressure to perform to a degree that I believe has never before been seen in U.S. education. Achievement levels must rise, so the number-one priority in schools is raising test scores, which is not necessarily equivalent to providing a world-class education. We have become a test prep/test score culture: If a school's scores are up and adequate yearly progress (AYP) has been met, the school is considered high-performing. The only pressure is to maintain the status quo. If, however, AYP has not been met, there is tremendous pressure on the school to improve in order to avoid sanctions in the form of negative press when test scores are published; reorganization of the school, which could include the transfer of teachers and administrators; and an inordinate amount of school-level planning throughout the course of the school year.

In my ongoing visits to schools, I get to see the panic and pressure up front and personal. I speak to educators who have thrown up their hands in frustration. Some have gone so far as to question whether or not they want to remain in the field of education. They feel that they have done all they can do and do not feel they can do any more.

One middle-aged white female teacher in an urban northeastern city spoke to me specifically about her 5th grade black males: She wanted so badly for them to be successful, but she felt she just wasn't getting through to them. As we conversed, she began to cry. She was hurting inside. She told me that she loved her kids, but that she had simply run out of strategies to reach them. She said that her students had severe behavioral problems. I told her that I would like to visit her classroom the next day, when the students returned. I suspected much of her problem was due to the climate and culture of her classroom and perhaps even the whole school. I wanted to get a bird's-eye view of what the climate and culture looked like when she and her students were in the room.

When I walked into this teacher's classroom, I immediately noticed a major problem with her classroom climate and culture. The room was chaotic and lacked organization, the walls were practically bare, and there was no clear evidence that the teacher was in charge. Many names were written on the board for after-school detention; several had a string of check marks beside their names. Looking at the students, I could literally see the brilliance in each of their eyes. I knew they were smart and that they had the potential for greatness. The problem was that the teacher focused too much on discipline and not enough on climate and culture.

What do we mean by *climate* and *culture*? I have studied school and classroom climate very intently and have read many different definitions of the term, which can be reduced to a single word: *mood*. When I analyze the climate of a given school or classroom, I am essentially gauging how the overall feeling and tone of the environment affects the teachers' ability to teach and the students' ability to learn. School and classroom culture can also be reduced to a single word: *lifestyle*. When I analyze the culture of a given school or classroom, I am essentially gauging how the overall way of life of the environment affects teachers and students. When I assess the combined climate and culture of a school or of individual classrooms, I want to gauge what the students see, hear, feel, and experience there and whether the learning environment fosters the proper attitude and decision making necessary for student success.

How Climate and Culture Affect Bullying

In schools and districts throughout the United States, heightened attention has been given to the problem of bullying. Stakeholders are increasingly being held accountable for detecting it, and consequences have become increasingly severe. Climate and culture determine whether bullying can take root in a classroom or school. The climate and culture can boldly state either that bullying is not allowed or that it is acceptable.

Climate and culture will speak to even the most subtle forms of bullying. For example, I can recall a student who appeared to fit in with everyone, but would never go to the cafeteria to eat with her peers. She would instead go to the library and read, pretty much every day. I didn't think much of it initially and concluded that this student simply wanted to read. However, upon further investigation, I discovered that the student didn't want to be in the cafeteria because her attire was a constant source of ridicule. She did not wear the latest styles and brands, and her peers would tease her about it. I later learned that she was also being teased in classrooms, but that this went undetected by her teachers. This situation was a function of the climate and culture of my school; in order to ameliorate it, I myself as principal needed to address it, as did the teachers in their classrooms. By addressing the problem and demonstrating to my students and staff that it was being taken seriously, we were in a much better position to get a handle on it and favorably affect the overall climate and culture of the school.

It works the same way with you in your classroom: *You must make it a priority to ensure a welcoming climate and culture for the sake of your students' academic success.* The mood of your classroom affects whether or not your students can learn at optimal levels—what your students see, hear, feel, and experience in your classroom will determine academic outcomes. Great instruction alone will not yield the results you desire for your students. You must pay close attention to the overall learning environment as well.

The Importance of What Students See, Hear, Feel, and Experience in the Classroom

During a postobservation conference with the 5th grade teacher whose classroom I visited, we began by focusing on what the students *saw* when they walked into her room—the seating arrangement, the walls, the bulletin boards, the overall use of classroom space, the teacher herself, and the other students. What statements did each of these observations make to the students?

Next, we examined what the students *heard*. What kinds of initial interactions occurred between the teacher and students? What kinds of greetings took place? How did the teacher typically speak to the students, and in what tone? What kinds of interactions occurred among students? Were they cordial, orderly, and productive? Was there evidence of caring and compassion? What kind of language was used? What was considered acceptable and unacceptable speech?

We then examined what the students might *feel* as they entered the classroom. What emotions did they experience? Was the classroom a relaxed environment? Was it conducive to learning? Did students appear comfortable? Was there a possibility that bullying existed in the environment that the teacher may not be aware of? Did the students feel valued, appreciated, and respected in this environment? Did they feel safe and free from harassment? Did they feel good about themselves?

Finally, we examined the overall *experience* of the classroom. What was it like to be a student in this classroom? Was this an environment that the students looked forward to being in every day? Was instruction student-centered? Was it rigorous? Was learning occurring? What kind of impression did the experience have on the students? Were students able to learn without peer pressure to conform to counterproductive expectations? There is still an unspoken notion in far too many classrooms among children of color that to be smart is to be "acting white." The classroom experience must encourage students to display their intelligence without risking repercussions from their classmates.

As the teacher and I conversed, it became clear to me that she thought she had a classroom management problem. She felt that her students could not sit still quietly long enough to learn in her classroom and that she had run out of ideas to remedy this problem. Whenever a student broke her classroom rules, which was often, she would write the student's name on the board. For repeat infractions, she would write check marks next to the name. Halfway through the class period, several students would already have several checks next to their name. This strategy backfired, however, as it was equivalent to putting the students' names in lights: These were the students who received all of the teacher's attention. Students who persisted in misbehaving despite having check marks next to their names were sent to the vice principal's office, which could result in suspensions.

Getting Students to Drop Their Masks

I remind educators often that many children arrive at school wearing invisible masks. Many teachers spend entire careers teaching to masks instead of to children, either because they aren't aware of the masks or because they haven't figured out how to get students to take them off. These masks are the result of peer pressure, which leads students to put their guard up and to pretend that they are something they're not. The only way to effectively remove the masks is to ensure a positive classroom climate and culture.

It was not acceptable for the students whose classroom I visited to exhibit their innate brilliance. In their minds, they had to act out because this is what they were expected to do; this is how they expected each other to behave; this was their mask. The teacher's challenge, then, was to either remove the masks or to create a learning environment that would permit the students to remove the masks themselves.

My oldest son, also named Baruti, recently graduated *magna cum laude* from college. The contrast between his high school years and his college years is enormous. I was quite familiar with his high school: It was a stereotypical urban high school in northern New Jersey. I watched my son put on "the mask" every day throughout his high school years. It had nothing to do with academic success; the mask he wore enabled him to survive the rigors of a counterproductive school climate and culture.

In schools such as my son's, it's not the academic coursework that yields the greatest challenge for students, but rather the rigors of a climate and culture that force students to conform to peer pressure so that they can cope day to day. As a result, Baruti was an average student at best. It was virtually impossible for him to focus on academics because the school climate and culture required him to wear a mask and to always be cognizant that he was wearing it. By contrast, when he went on to college, he could be his brilliant self; he did not have to wear the mask any longer. The result was that he graduated near the top of his graduating class.

My youngest son, Jabari, had a very similar experience. When he got to high school, the climate and culture of the school forced him to adapt to its negative environment. Whenever I visited the school, it was clear to me that climate and culture issues prevented the male students in particular from exhibiting their brilliance. The students pressured each other to conform to expected behaviors. All of them put on their masks in the morning and kept them on throughout high school. As with Baruti, Jabari did just enough to complete high school but did not go that extra mile. And yet, when he got to college, he excelled. Why? The climate and culture pressures that he experienced at the high school did not exist in college. He could now remove the mask without having to look over his shoulder.

It is my firm contention that the stakeholders of a school possess the power, influence, and authority to favorably affect the school's climate and culture. It starts with the leadership and trickles throughout the building. But you can't correct a problem if you do not recognize that it exists. To acknowledge discipline or classroom management issues without seeing the bigger picture of climate and culture is totally detrimental to the school.

In your school and in your classroom, the focus must be on establishing a climate and culture in which students can check their masks at the door. If they have to wear their masks on their walk or bus ride to and from school, that is understandable—it may not be right, but knowing the realities of inner-city life, it is understandable. The key is establishing a building-level climate and culture. And attitude goes hand-in-glove with climate and culture: Think of attitude as being equivalent to an automobile, with climate and culture being a tunnel. On the other side is your destination: closure of the achievement gap.

Poverty and the Attitude Gap

In workshops, I frequently ask my audiences to tell me what they think the main reason is that so many urban and rural schools are underperforming. Wherever I am, the answer is always the same: *poverty*. Educators all over the country feel that poverty is a major obstacle to urban and rural student achievement. If it weren't for poverty, children in urban and rural schools would be excelling.[1]

Although poverty is a variable that cannot be ignored, I have held the position for quite some time that it is not a legitimate excuse for failure or underachievement. As a classroom teacher, you have no control over poverty; you cannot change the conditions that your students might be going home to every day. At best, you can inspire your students to one day rise above their situation, but you cannot change it, so it makes little sense to dwell on it or make it an excuse. I remind teachers all the time that in our own job interviews as teachers, we never blame poverty or use it as an excuse; we simply lay out the case that we are the right ones for the job. We must apply that same level of confidence to our students.

Because poverty is a variable that we cannot do anything about, our energy must be devoted to those areas where we have absolute control—the climate and culture of the classroom. The classroom teacher is in a position to create an oasis for students: Whatever is going on in their lives outside of school can be left outside, and the students can look forward every morning to a day of productive learning.

---

[1] A number of high-poverty schools are bucking the odds and doing extraordinarily well throughout the United States, providing an assortment of lessons for turning high-poverty schools into high-performing schools. For more information, see Jensen (2009) and Parrett and Budge (2012).

If poverty is allowed to be made an excuse for underachievement, students don't stand a chance. *You* are the number one determinant of your students' success. *You* are the difference maker. *You* are the game changer.

A Framework for Closing the Attitude Gap

In an effort to systematize the process of creating a climate and culture conducive to closing the attitude gap, I have developed a framework comprised of the following five strands:

1. **Attitude toward students (do I believe in them?)**—This strand focuses on the teacher's *attitude* toward his or her students. You cannot effectively teach and inspire students if you do not believe in them.

2. **Relationship with students (do I know them?)**—This strand focuses on the teacher's *relationship* with his or her students. You cannot effectively teach and inspire students if you do not know them.

3. **Compassion for students (do I care about them?)**—This strand focuses on the teacher's *care, concern,* and *compassion* for his or her students. You cannot effectively teach and inspire students if you do not care about them.

4. **Environment for learning (do I provide my students with an environment of excellence?)**—This strand focuses on the *classroom environment* that the teacher has created. You cannot effectively teach and inspire students if the classroom environment is not conducive to learning.

5. **Relevance in instruction (do I realize who my students are?)**—This strand focuses on *culturally responsive* teaching and learning. You cannot effectively teach and inspire students if you do not take into account who they are historically and culturally.

The remaining chapters of this book will examine each of these strands in depth.

2 | **Attitude Toward Students**
Do I Believe in Them?

REFLECTIVE QUESTIONS

Before reading this chapter, look into a mirror and ask yourself the following questions about your students:

1. Do I believe in them?

2. Do I have a passion for teaching them?

3. Do I have a purpose for teaching them?

4. Do I treat teaching them as a mission?

5. Do I have a vision for what I expect of them?

6. Do I set incremental and long-range goals for them to achieve?

7. Do I plan each day thoroughly toward their success?

8. Do I see myself as a role model for them and always conduct myself as a professional?

9. Do I see myself as the number-one determinant of their success or failure?

10. Do I conduct daily self-reflections and self-assessments of my practice of teaching them?

In July of 2006, as I was preparing for my second year as principal of Newark Tech, I received a phone call. It was the principal of an elementary school in Montgomery, Alabama; she wanted me to conduct a professional development workshop for her staff.

I had wanted to visit Montgomery for a long time, given its place in civil rights history. I wanted to get down there and take all of that history in—to visit Rosa Parks' bus stop, the Rosa Parks Museum, Dr. Martin Luther King's first church, and the King family house. Above all else, I wanted to see and stand on the Edmund Pettus Bridge in Selma, a little over 50 miles away from Montgomery. I told the principal that I would go down to Montgomery if she promised to take me to the Edmund Pettus Bridge immediately following my presentation. She understood why and said of course. She requested my services for August 28, 2006—the 43rd anniversary of the March on Washington.

Once the workshop was completed, a couple of teachers and I immediately jumped into the principal's car and drove along

Highway 80 to Selma. As we drove, all I could think about were the marchers who had marched along that same highway in March of 1965, demanding their right to vote. It all began on the Edmund Pettus Bridge, where the original 600 marchers were attacked and beaten on March 7, 1965. I needed to stand on that bridge that day. I needed to walk on that same sidewalk and feel the emotions that the marchers had felt.

Once we arrived at the bridge, I asked the principal and the teachers to allow me some time to myself. I walked the sidewalk that the marchers walked, and when I got to the center of the bridge, I stood there in deep reflection. I thought about what had transpired on the bridge back in 1965, of course, but I also reflected deeply on my practice as an educator and principal. I began to question my attitude toward my students. I thought to myself that what I do as an educator pales in comparison to what took place on that bridge; that if those men and women could endure what they endured on that historic day, I could at least take a young mind and mold it into greatness through effective motivation, education, and empowerment.

As I stood on that bridge, three questions came to my mind that I felt compelled to answer then and there:

- Principal Kafele, who are you?
- Principal Kafele, what are you about?
- Principal Kafele, what is your most recent evidence?

For almost an hour, I pondered these questions as they related to my attitude toward my students and my overall practice as an educator. It was as though I was engaged in a reflective exercise relative to my mission while standing on the Edmund Pettus Bridge. I will expound on the answers to my three questions at the end of this chapter.

When I returned to New Jersey, I purchased a mirror for every staff member employed at Newark Tech. At our first staff meeting that September, I challenged staff to stand up one at a time, look at themselves in the mirror, and ask themselves out loud the same three questions I'd asked myself on the bridge. I asked them to answer each question aloud as well. This became quite an emotional experience; several of the teachers began to cry while answering the first question as they looked deeply within themselves. I subsequently encouraged my staff members to hang their mirrors somewhere in their classrooms and to ask themselves the three reflective questions on a daily basis as a ritual every morning to mentally prepare for the day.

Since my trip to Selma, not a day has gone by that I don't look into my mirror and ask myself those same three reflective questions. I have found that this practice has made me a much better educator because it has forced me to reflect upon and assess my practice on a daily basis.

Believing in Your Students

To develop a climate and culture conducive to closing the attitude gap, it is absolutely crucial that you believe in your students and demonstrate your belief in them regularly (Ladson-Billings, 1994). You must believe in *all* your students, regardless of their circumstances or any "baggage" they may bring along with them to school. When you look into their eyes, you must see brilliance looking back at you. You must see a reflection of yourself looking back at you. You must see a student who is destined for greatness as a direct result of the unwavering belief that you have in him or her. How can we expect children to perform at optimal levels if we lack the belief that they can do so? Our belief in our students increases the probability that they will believe in themselves.

Belief in our students' ability to soar should translate to setting high standards and expectations for them (Edwards, 2010). I recall attending a parent-teacher conference for my daughter, Kibriya, when she was in 7th grade. The teacher seemed quite pleased with the fact that Kibriya was getting a *C* in his class. I could not believe what I was hearing. On the one hand, I was disappointed with Kibriya, and with myself for allowing her to underperform. On the other hand, I was disappointed with the teacher for feeling that a *C* was satisfactory. I told him that such a grade was unacceptable in my household. The teacher's comments demonstrated to me that his standards and expectations for my daughter—and perhaps for the entire class—were low, and that he did not believe in Kibriya's ability to do significantly better. I wondered if he saw in my daughter a potentially high-performing student or if he only saw an average student and therefore pushed her only to perform at a *C* level. I wondered if he believed in her.

If you are going to successfully close the attitude gap in your classroom, not only must you believe in your students, but you must also ensure that they believe in themselves and in their own ability to achieve excellence. Far too many students go to school every day lacking a belief in their ability to achieve at the highest levels, leading directly to the low levels of achievement in reading and math that we see in urban and rural schools. In urban centers in particular, students are contending with multiple distractions as well.

When I taught 4th and 6th grades, my students produced amazing results. Most of them genuinely liked school—they wanted to be there and looked forward to showing up every morning. They were eager to be in my classroom every day because they knew that I believed in them. After those students went on to high school, I got back in touch with several who had subsequently become honor students. They all said the same thing: *You believed in me.*

Demonstrating Belief in Your Students

It is vital that your students *know* that you believe in them. It is one thing to say that you do, but it's something different and far more powerful to convince your students that yes, you really do believe in them. You must find excuses to articulate this to them. You cannot assume that they know.

Over the years, I have asked many urban and rural students when the last time they heard someone say that they believed in them was. The students typically look puzzled and say, "Never." So many children are unaccustomed to hearing people tell them that they believe in them. Just imagine if they heard this regularly from their parents, teachers, counselors, principal, and so on—it would make a tremendous difference in the way that they see themselves.

A Passion for Teaching

Having passion for teaching is a game-changer. It implies that you want success deeply; that you want it badly; that you will do anything for it; that you will not settle for anything less; that anything less than your absolute best is simply unacceptable. Take a look into your mirror. Is the individual looking back at you passionate about teaching? About children? About growing professionally?

People become teachers for many different reasons; unfortunately, one of those reasons is because there are no other jobs available. Consider the following scenario. An individual—let's call him Mr. J.—has a bachelor's degree in finance, but there are simply no jobs available to him. He is aware of a teaching shortage in a nearby school district, so he applies for a position. He studies for and passes a written examination to teach math and gets his provisional certification. He subsequently gets hired as a math teacher in a low-performing urban middle school. The school population is 55 percent black and 45 percent Latino. Ninety percent of the students receive free or reduced-price lunch. Performance rates are traditionally low and suspension rates are traditionally high, particularly for the male population. The high school on-time graduation rate in this district is at 60 percent for girls and 40 percent for boys. The student population is highly transient and the majority of the households are headed by single parents—typically by the mother. The surrounding community has a heavy gang presence, drug use and drug selling abound, and crime and violence rates are very high.

Before going further, let me note that I have deliberately chosen not to assign a racial identity to Mr. J. Twenty years ago, I certainly would have—I would have made him white, to underline the difference in backgrounds between him and his students. Although I am well aware that children of color need role models whom they can relate to, I am convinced that the racial identity of a teacher just doesn't matter. What matters to me is whether or not that teacher has a passion for teaching, a passion for children, and a passion for growing professionally. As long as the teacher has these three essential characteristics, everything else will follow.

Let's go back to Mr. J. He's walking into a high-needs situation on his first day. This is not just a job—it's a mission. What he's about to embark upon will affect the life of every child he teaches. Despite the challenges that the school faces and the fact that he has never taught a day in his life, Mr. J. is expected to perform. The question, then, becomes, "Is he passionate about teaching? Specifically, is he passionate about teaching urban children of color, since they make up the population of his school?" This question about ethnicity is the proverbial 800-pound elephant in the room; few want to address it, but it must be addressed, and in earnest. If Mr. J. wants to help close the attitude gap of his students, he must develop a passion for teaching urban children of color.

Additionally, does Mr. J. want success for his students badly? Does he truly want his children to soar? Is he willing to give them his all? Is he willing to do all that he has to do in order to ensure that his students are successful? Does he have a burning desire to get the job done? Is he passionate about ensuring that high-quality instruction will occur in his classroom every day? If so, as a new teacher, how will he make that happen? All teachers should ask themselves these questions.

On his first day, it would be hard to tell how passionate Mr. J. is about teaching. After all, not only is he a new teacher, but he also chose teaching because he couldn't get a job in his field. He's therefore coming into something that he had not envisioned for himself. If his students are going to be optimally successful in his classroom, in addition to all of the pedagogical skills that he must acquire, he must develop a passion for the work—a passion that is more than evident to his students.

A Passion for Children

Mr. J. must not only be passionate about teaching; he must also be passionate about children. He teaches children first, subjects second. I have come across many educators who are passionate about their content areas, but don't especially like children. Of course, none of them have ever admitted this to me, but it comes across loud and clear in conversations and observations. As one of my principal colleagues is known to say, every child deserves a teacher who is absolutely crazy about them. Mr. J. must be passionate; he needs to genuinely like and care about the students he is going to teach. His passion for them will come across in the level of dedication and compassion that he brings to them daily.

Are you passionate about the students you teach? Do you genuinely like children? Do you want deeply for them to be successful? Are you willing to invest in them the same level of energy and commitment that you would your own children? Your children require your best. They require your unwavering and uncompromising commitment, despite the odds and despite the challenges they are faced with daily. When they get the best "you," their chances for success increase exponentially.

A Passion for Professional Growth

Mr. J. will be teaching for the first time in his life, and yet he knows nothing about teaching. He knows his content—in this case, mathematics—but he doesn't really know about teaching it to middle school students. How is he going to connect with his students so that he can teach them? How is he going to close the attitude gap? Mr. J. must want to grow professionally. He must truly desire to become an extraordinary educator. If his students stand any chance for success, he must evolve pedagogically. He must therefore be passionate about his own professional growth and development. He must welcome it with enthusiasm.

As educators, we cannot assume that one size fits all. We must grow professionally, but we must seek professional development opportunities that clearly address the students we are teaching. If you happen to have urban or rural children at risk of failure in your classroom, and it has become evident that their academic needs are not being met, then it is incumbent upon you to seek professional development that addresses the academic needs of these particular children. Inherent in seeking help must be the passion to get it done. You must have a passion to learn as much as you can and to successfully implement that which you learn.

I would be remiss if I didn't mention that passion cannot be taught, which is why I will not offer any suggestions for developing passion. I speak so often about having the will and the passion to teach, but these are qualities that one must simply possess; they can be either tapped into or unleashed, but they can't be taught. These two qualities really distinguish those who truly want to be in the classroom and those who do not. If you have the passion and the will to close the attitude gap of your students, that gap will be closed. You must therefore return to your mirror and ask yourself if you have the will and the passion to make it happen for your students.

A Purpose for Teaching

When it comes to meeting very specific objectives, purpose is a very powerful concept. Your purpose tells the world what you're about and what your intentions are. Many do not even have to state their purpose; it becomes evident in their deeds and actions.

So, what is your purpose for teaching? In other words, why do you do it? What drives you to get up every morning and report to your school and teach your students? Does your purpose drive everything that you say and do in your classroom? Does it define who you are as a classroom teacher? The probability for success increases exponentially for educators who are driven by a purpose. Your purpose drives you as it shapes you.

In my professional development workshops, I typically ask educators whether or not they've defined their purpose for teaching. In most cases, less than half of them have taken the time to define why they do what they do—in other words, they have not given definition to their practice. For my part, when I started as a teacher back in 1988, my core purpose was to teach my 5th grade students their story—meaning their history. Most of my students were black, and I was aware that they knew little about black history. I, however, understood the powerful effect that knowing this history would have on how they perceived themselves, so I made it a point to teach them about the historic contributions of black individuals to every subject that I taught. Exposing my students to this rich history made learning highly relevant to them and enabled me to teach according to my purpose.

What is your purpose as it relates to closing the attitude gap in your classroom? Remember, the attitude gap is defined as *the gap between those students who have the will to strive for academic excellence and those who do not.* How will you close this gap? How will you encourage a child to develop the will to excel? Your own purpose will play a big part, particularly if it's focused on motivating your students to succeed.

I meet so many teachers who are simply at a loss. They describe for me how difficult home conditions and dangerous neighborhoods affect the drive and conduct of their students. To the layperson, changing these students' attitudes seems like an overwhelming if not impossible challenge. To the teacher with a purpose, however, the challenge is not so daunting because *it is an inherent part of her purpose*—it is the reason she reports to work every day in the first place.

Toward developing your purpose, find that quiet place in your home or your classroom. Consider why you do what you do. Reflect upon your initial motivation for becoming a classroom teacher. Consider the challenges that your students face. Consider what you want your students to achieve as a result of being in your class. Consider where you want your students to be long term. As you reflect upon these points, begin to define your role: Just as every word in a dictionary has a definition, so, too, should your role as a teacher be defined. Write the definition down and share it with your students, parents, colleagues, and administrators. Let them know that this is who you are and what you are about, and that nothing and no one will stand in the way of you fulfilling your purpose for your students.

Treating Teaching as a Mission

Treating teaching as a mission is a powerful aspect of my framework for closing the attitude gap. As a principal, I'll take a mission-oriented teacher over a career-oriented one any day. The teacher with a mission orientation is going to get the job done; nothing is going to stop her from achieving the goal of student success. Although teaching is her career, she believes there's more to it. Through her mission orientation, she is essentially saying to her students, "Your success in my classroom is my mission. Your future is my mission. Your life is my mission. And my mission will be accomplished." A teacher with a mission orientation is bound to have higher expectations for all of her students than a career-oriented teacher.

As I mentioned in the introduction, I began writing this book by retreating to a hotel for a week so that I would not be distracted by the happenings of the world. During that week, I learned of a rash of murders in Newark, where most of the students I've worked with over the past several years are from. Many of my students have been affected by these murders. How are they going to want to excel in school when there are so many young people dying around them? How can we expect them to flourish academically when they have to be concerned not only about their own safety, but about that of their friends and loved ones? Teachers have to understand these dynamics and be concerned about them, but they must also have strategies in place to help students overcome their circumstances. Their attitude cannot simply be one of "I teach science" or "I teach math"; it must, rather, be one of "I teach children who are faced with enormous challenges that adversely affect their attitudes toward school, but I will make sure that nothing inhibits my students from experiencing success in my classroom. I'm on a mission and I will not stop until the mission is accomplished."

A school's mission statement should reflect its teachers' mission orientation. During my workshops, I ask teachers to stand

and recite their school mission statements. In most cases, they can't—they don't know them. I also ask if any of the teachers have written classroom mission statements; usually they haven't. However, both types of mission statements are critically important.

Imagine, if you will, a teacher whose mission it is to close the attitude gap among her students. She has written and posted a classroom mission statement that supports her mission orientation. Now imagine that this teacher requires all of her students to recite the mission statement each day and expects them to learn it by heart. Here we have a recipe for some serious learning: Not only has the teacher expressed her personal mission, but the classroom itself does as well, and students are expected to know it. Steps have been put in place for these students to soar despite the challenges that they face. (I discuss classroom mission statements further in Chapter 5.)

Developing a Vision of What to Expect from Students

You must be able to envision where your students will be as a result of the instruction you provide and the interactions that you have with them on a daily basis. At the start of the school year, you've got to ask yourself, "What will my students have achieved by the end of each marking period? What effect will my instruction and interactions have on them over the course of the entire school year? How successful will my students be in the long term as a result of having me as their teacher?" The answers to these questions will supply the vision of what you expect from your students. Having a sense of vision for your students' academic growth and development is powerful: It enables you to already "see" their success before you utter the first word of the first lesson or they complete their first homework assignment.

Vision is seeing, anticipating, and expecting an intended outcome. Coming to school with a day-to-day mindset is simply not good enough. You have got to visualize your students achieving at the highest levels because you are their teacher, and you have to project this vision. In my interactions with teachers across the country, I have come across far too many who lack vision either for their own or their students' success. Because of the enormous social and economic challenges that many of their students face, these teachers find it difficult to envision their students' success over the long haul. I remind them that excuses for their students' failure are unacceptable. *There are no excuses.*

I once worked with a teacher at a school who won a "Teacher of the Year" award an unprecedented eight times. She was a special needs teacher, but she didn't see her students' disabilities as handicaps or setbacks, and she certainly didn't see them as excuses. She envisioned her students doing great things despite their disabilities and she acted upon her vision. The result was success for her students and recognition for her. This teacher had a purpose; she was on a mission; and she had a vision for her and her students' success.

Imagine the power of telling your students that you already see their success—and of them believing you. You have got to tell them regularly that they will in fact achieve success in your classroom because you have already envisioned it happening. In addition to the short-term vision you have of your students' success in the school year, you must also share with them your long-term vision of them graduating from high school and college.

Too many children lack vision for themselves. They do not see beyond today; they do not dream big. Too many of them see so much death and destruction around them that it becomes almost impossible for them to envision life as an adult. This is where you come in: You must dare your students to envision themselves 10, 20, 30 years from now, achieving their dreams.

Just as you should have school and classroom mission statements, so, too, should you have school and classroom vision statements. As with mission statements, I ask teachers in my workshops to recite either their school or classroom vision statements and rarely get any volunteers. Vision statements are powerful because they tell students where you expect them to be as a result of the instruction and interactions that occur in your classroom. I cannot overstate the importance of you having a vision for your students' success in your classroom. You must share your classroom vision statement with students often. (I discuss classroom vision statements further in Chapter 5.)

Setting Short- and Long-Term Goals for Students

What concrete, short-term goals have you set for yourself that help fulfill your vision for your students? Consider the honor roll, for example: Of the students in your class or classes, how many are currently on the honor roll? Whatever the number, I am quite sure that you can increase it. How will you do so? Additional goals can include increasing the number of students who

- Consistently complete homework assignments.
- Pass quizzes and tests with an *A* or *B* grade.
- Meet the criteria for "Student of the Week/Month."
- Engage in extracurricular activities.
- Maintain perfect attendance.
- Arrive to school or class on time.

What's key is to actually let your students know that you've set such goals, ideally by posting them on the wall or a bulletin board. Doing this increases the likelihood that students will be encouraged to help meet the goals. Posting goals also clearly demonstrates to your students that you are serious about them, because it shows them that you measure your success by their performance in your classroom. In addition to short-term goals, you should also set long-term goals—increasing the number of students who will make the honor roll in all four marking periods, for example, or the number who will maintain perfect attendance for the entire school year. (In Chapter 5, I will discuss goal setting from the vantage point of the students.)

Planning Each Day Thoroughly for Students' Success

Planning is essential, unavoidable, and nonnegotiable. You must have a plan for all of your students if you want to maximize their potential in your classroom. In special needs classrooms, teachers are required to devise individual education plans (IEPs) for each of their students. This makes sense, because each student has his or her own unique needs; the likelihood of student success increases exponentially when there is a plan in place. For this reason, I believe that teachers in all classes should plan for each of their students separately. I am well aware that this requires additional, time-consuming work, but I can see no other way to effectively close the attitude gap.

I often ask teachers whether they devised concrete goals or wrote out a plan before embarking on their quest to become educators. Many say that they did. I then speak with them about the importance of well-written action plans in the world of business, and remind them that the same holds true in education: students also need well-written plans tailored to their learning styles. *Whenever there are two or more students in a classroom, there will be a need to differentiate instruction.*

I can recall vividly the effects of one-size-fits-all teaching when I was a high school student. From class to class and year to year, instruction was typically delivered via lecture, and we either got it or didn't. Such lessons did not take into consideration how the students actually learned; teachers simply assumed that all students were auditory learners. If students didn't comprehend the lesson, teachers just assumed that they hadn't studied hard enough. If my teachers had paused to consider the unique learning styles of their students and planned for instruction accordingly, I am quite certain that we would have enjoyed a much more productive school experience.

Being a Role Model for Students and Conducting Yourself Professionally

During a typical school day, children can be with their teachers for upwards of seven hours. Multiply that number by the number of school days in a year, and you'll see what a substantial amount of time children spend with their teachers. As a consequence, teachers become role models for their students whether they accept it or not.

I like to tell teachers that *power is within their hands*—the power to effect enormous change in the lives of students, the power to create entire classrooms of high performers. There are many intangibles that we sometimes take for granted but that can have a huge effect on students' lives. One of those intangibles is the way that we conduct ourselves. Children are watching us, they admire us, and they are going to pick up some of our traits. We must always be cognizant of this and conduct ourselves as professionals at all times.

Do you see yourself as a role model for your students? Do you see yourself as having qualities that they may want to emulate? Do you realize that your students are watching you and listening to you? Aspects of *you* are slowly but surely becoming aspects of *them*, too. We must be mindful of how we speak, what we say, and how we dress. So many students are actively looking for role models. We must be conscious of living up to their expectations.

We are not just role models when we're in school with students; we are role models 24/7. We could easily bump into students while out shopping or attending a community event. Our students have certain expectations for us. We can't be seen as totally different people outside of school. Once students grant us their trust and respect, it becomes our obligation to live up to it whenever and wherever students may see us. As a teacher and a principal, I always told my students that I was the same person outside of school as I was inside. This was important to me. I embraced my status as a role model and was always mindful of the fact that I was modeling expected outcomes. (Of course, our students may not always tell us that they hold us in high regard. Not long ago, a recently graduated student of mine tweeted that I was a role model to all the male students at our school. This message was then retweeted several times. Although I had a rapport and relationship with the student, this was the first time I learned that he viewed me as a role model.)

When I visit schools in my role as consultant, it always makes me feel good to see teachers dressed in their business or professional attire. It speaks volumes about who they are and the image they want to project for their students. These educators clearly understand that they are role models and that they are being watched and admired by their students. I also pay attention to the way teachers speak to their students; I want to hear that they are modeling the right stuff. What we say and how we say it will influence the way students speak back to us. We cannot speak to them as if they were simply our friends—that's a boundary that we must not cross or allow our students to cross. We are professionals, and our intent must be to bring our students closer to where *we* are, not to go where *they* are in the name of forging a connection.

I have been to schools where teachers, leaders, and students do not greet one another in the morning; they just walk past one another without acknowledging each other's presence. This speaks volumes about the climate and culture of the school. As role models, it is incumbent upon us to take the initiative and greet our students—and to expect that they will greet us back. In my own role as a principal, whenever I noticed a lack of greetings at a new school, I would address it immediately either during our morning convocations or over the PA system.

Do you see yourself as a role model? Do you always conduct yourself as a professional? Are you intentional about modeling expected outcomes? It is absolutely essential that you are.

Being the Primary Determinant of Your Students' Success or Failure

The idea that you as a teacher are the number-one determinant of your students' success or failure generates a lot of conversation in my workshops. Teachers say to me, "Wait a minute, Principal Kafele: You expect me to believe that, of all the variables in my students' lives, I'm the single one that will determine whether or not my kids succeed?" My answer is an emphatic, unequivocal "*Yes.*"

I recall one teacher I spoke with who couldn't make this leap. He felt that the negative influences in the community outside of his school were entirely too strong for him to overcome. I was well aware of the dynamics of the community, which is precisely why I felt that he needed to change his attitude toward his students: If he succumbed to his belief that he was helpless in the face of negative outside influences, then his students did not stand a chance—*they were already at a deficit because of his attitude toward them.*

Teachers will say to me, "Principal Kafele, you don't know our kids. We're different here. We have got to be the worst district in the United States!" I can't tell you how many places I have visited where the overriding sentiment was, "We are the worst!" Well, if that's the mentality of the staff in the building, how can we realistically expect the students to achieve? Those kids are doomed! The mindset must be that despite the social challenges, our students are going to soar like eagles, because *we* are their teachers.

At-risk urban and rural children in particular need teachers who are confident about their ability to effectively and properly educate them. They need teachers who see social challenges not as excuses for inaction, but as motivation to help students scale previously unimagined heights. The presence of drugs, violence, or crime in a community should motivate teachers to keep students clean, safe, and lawful. Additionally, teachers should make their students understand that they and their peers have a role to play in eradicating the ills that plague their community—and that the best way of doing so is by working hard in school.

You must be confident that you can help your students overcome the odds. They deserve the opportunity to be successful,
and the best way of ensuring their success is by declaring that it
will happen, because *you* are their teacher.

What is your attitude toward your students? How do you feel
about them and their chances for success in life? What is your
attitude about your ability to inspire them to strive for excellence? The answers to these questions will determine outcomes
for your students.

When I was a principal at Newark Tech, if I was standing in
front of the school during student dismissal, I would sometimes direct my students' attention to the sign on the front
of the building. "Read the sign aloud," I would say, and they
would respond, "Newark Tech." I would then ask them if they
could see anything else. "There is another name there, but you
don't see it," I'd say. "There is an invisible sign, and it reads
'Principal Kafele.'" You see, I was well aware that if my school
was underperforming, then the community would see me, the
principal, as a failure. I therefore accepted that, as principal, I
was the number-one determinant of the success or failure of
Newark Tech. The school was going to go as I went.

The exact same principle applies to you as the classroom
teacher. Your name is on that classroom door—literally, in
most cases. That is *your* classroom. *You* are the one who deter-
mines outcomes in that classroom. *You* are the one who creates scholars in that classroom—who creates hope, who lets
dreams flourish, who keeps negative influences from entering

the room. You remind your students constantly that where they are now doesn't necessarily determine where they will wind up later.

Daily Self-Reflections and Self-Assessments

Given the continuous pressures and demands to perform at optimal levels in the classroom, how do you ensure that you are consistently displaying the right attitude toward your students? As I mentioned earlier in this chapter, I think it is very important to pause and reflect upon your performance in front of a mirror on a daily basis. Not a single day should go by that you do not do this. At the end of every school day, you must run the mental DVD of your entire day, from the moment you set foot on school grounds until all of your students had left the building. Think of your state of mind when you arrived at school in the morning. Think of the lessons you presented. Think of the interactions you had with your students. Think of how you challenged and engaged them. Think of any incidents that may have occurred and how you handled them. During your reflection time, you should also assess your performance: Rate yourself, and be brutally honest. Ask yourself what adjustments you might need to make. You should not have to wait for an evaluator to rate your performance.

After going through your self-reflection and self-assessment, you may want to jot down some goals related to what you'd like to improve upon for the next day, preferably in a journal reserved for this purpose. Write your goals down along with your strategies for meeting them. At the start of the next day, complete the reflection process by returning to your mirror and asking yourself the three questions I introduced at the beginning of this chapter:

- Who are you?
- What are you about?
- What is your most recent evidence?

I strongly recommend that all educators get themselves a small mirror, hang it on the wall of their classroom or office, and post these three questions beneath it. When you arrive to your classroom or office, the first thing you should do is ask your reflection, "Who are you?" After doing this, wait for your reflection to answer. Yes, you read that correctly: *Wait for your reflection to answer.* The mirror never lies.

When I was the principal of Newark Tech, I'd go to my mirror every morning, look deep into my own eyes, and ask, "Principal Kafele, who are you?" I'd then wait for an answer. My reflection would usually answer along the following lines: "I am Principal Kafele of Newark Tech. I am not ordinary at what I do; I am *extraordinary* at what I do." If you're going to do your part to produce extraordinary results, you have to *feel* extraordinary as an educator. After all, how can you consider it realistic that you will achieve extraordinary results if you don't even know what "extraordinary" feels like?

The second question you need to ask yourself in the mirror is, "What are you about?" This is a question of purpose. When I used to ask this question, my reflection would typically answer as follows: "I am about the business of ensuring that every student in the building is striving to achieve excellence." In other words, my purpose was my students' success. You, too, must hear your reflection confirm that you are all about your students—all of them—and you will therefore do all that is necessary to ensure their academic success.

The third question you need to ask is, "What is your most recent evidence?" This is the toughest question; it is the moment of truth. This is the question that asks, as Janet Jackson once did, "What have you done for me lately?" What have you done in the past 24 hours to confirm that you are who you say you are? Determine what strategies, activities, and interactions you've engaged in to move your students closer to success.

Once you have heard your reflection respond to the third question, you are ready to start your day. If you have no good answer, you know that you have work to do—each and every day, you must be able to acknowledge something you did that day to move your students forward from where they were the day before.

I absolutely love the mirror activity. When I was a principal, it was a tremendous way for me to start my day every morning. It helped me to ensure that I was in the right state of mind for my students every day.

3 | Relationship with Students

Do I Know Them?

REFLECTIVE QUESTIONS

Before reading this chapter, look into a mirror and ask yourself the following questions about your students:

1. Do I know them?

2. Do I know how they learn?

3. Do I know how to keep them inspired about learning?

4. Do I know how to keep them motivated to excel?

5. Do I know their goals and aspirations?

6. Do I know their needs and interests?

7. Do I know their experiences and realities?

8. Do I know their challenges and obstacles?

9. Do I know their parents?

10. Do I know their neighborhoods?

In the summer of 2003, I assumed the leadership of a middle school in the city in which I was raised. Less than a week after my appointment, I received a letter from the New Jersey State Department of Education noting that the school had been designated as a "persistently dangerous school" under the No Child Left Behind (NCLB) act. Ours was one of only 50 schools across the entire country with this designation. Under NCLB, parents with children in persistently dangerous schools could opt to transfer them into another school within the district. I was consequently (and understandably) flooded with phone calls from nervous parents demanding transfers for their students. My response was to send out a letter to these parents asking that they hold on and hear me out first. I wanted to assure them that there was nothing dangerous about my school and that I would guarantee that their children would be safe. I invited them all to a meeting intended to allay their anxiety and to appeal to them to keep their children with me.

The parents came to my late August meeting in droves. They listened to what I had to say and I listened to their concerns. We dialogued constructively. I assured them that the way to get the school to where it needed to be was through relationship building within the school—that is, by building a true school family. The vast majority of the parents believed in me and kept their children in my school.

As soon as the kids came back to school that fall, I went to work. In addition to making aesthetic changes to the building (having the entire building painted with a fresh coat of white paint, for example, and posting positive affirmations on the hallway walls), I had to change the school's climate and culture by implementing the five strands discussed in this book. On the first day of school and every Monday morning thereafter, I met with students in the auditorium and reminded them of how great they were, how special they were, how brilliant they were. Every week I told them positive things about themselves that many of them didn't hear anywhere else. I talked to them about life and about setting and achieving their goals. These meetings were so powerful that the word was soon out. The superintendent and members of the New Jersey State Department of Education even attended a couple. Parents would attend in large numbers just to hear the Monday morning message and to see how the students reacted.

In time, I got to know all 650 of my students. School staff transformed the climate and culture of the school by stressing relationship building in the way we greeted students in the morning, interacted with them in the hallways, and ate lunch with them in the cafeteria. At the end of the year, I received word from the New Jersey State Department of Education: My school had been removed from the persistently dangerous list. We accomplished this in just one year, thanks largely to the power of cultivating relationships with students.

Show me a school where strong relationships do not exist and I'll show you an underperforming school. Show me a school where relationships are intentional, however, and I'll show you a school with unlimited potential. And make no mistake about it, these relationships should be reciprocal—the students should be able to get to know us as well as we get to know them. They should see that we are human and that there is more to our lives beyond teaching.

Knowing Your Students

Do you know each student? Do you *really know* each one? I don't mean as a name on your roster; I mean the total child. Do you know him? Do you know who he is after the dismissal bell? Do you know who she is on the walk or bus ride home from school? Do you know who he is in his neighborhood? Do you know who she is in her home? The answers to these questions all affect each student's ability to learn in your classroom—and I would dare say that many educators might have difficulty answering them. Many may not even see the significance of answering them; they may take the position that they cannot control what goes on outside of their classrooms. I would agree wholeheartedly with this assertion, but I would add that it is still incumbent upon you to take the initiative to learn about your students' lives outside school, as it has direct implications for what they do inside school.

You must form a rapport with your students—a process that might begin with examining the way you greet your students every day. Are you warm? Sincere? Intentional? Personal? Do you show your students that you are happy to see them? As Allen Mendler says, "It is best to personalize your greeting by including the student's name. Students appreciate knowing that their teacher knows who they are" (2001, pp. 23–24). You might also establish a rapport in front of the school, on the playground, or in the hallway, before school and after school.

Knowing How Your Students Learn

How do your students learn? How do you connect with them? Are they auditory learners? Visual? Tactile-kinesthetic? What is the best instructional methodology for connecting with all of the learners in your classroom? Do they all learn alike? Do the males learn like the females? Does culture play a role? Do home or neighborhood conditions influence your students' learning?

To this day, I cringe every time I walk into a classroom and see a teacher lecturing. Of course, I am ecstatic for the auditory learners in the room; my concern is for the other types of learners, who have to sit through lessons directed to the wrong side of their brains. I have argued for many years that, in far too many cases, students in special needs classrooms simply have learning styles that are misunderstood. Consider, for example, my son Baruti. Over a few years in elementary school, several of his teachers wanted desperately to have him evaluated for a learning disability. Being an educator myself, I knew he didn't have one—the problem was the instructional methodology of some of his teachers, which was highly lecture- and teacher-centered. As it turns out, Baruti is a visual learner. A voracious reader with an insatiable appetite for books and an unquenchable thirst for new knowledge, he underlines and outlines practically everything he reads. Instead of just reading the words on the page, he processes the information further using visual cues. As a result, he is now a walking encyclopedia.

Students, particularly those in urban and rural classrooms, need to be placed in student-centered environments where all of them are given the opportunity to learn based on their own unique learning styles. Of course, this requires a high degree of differentiated instruction. It also requires you to know your students, since getting to know them is the best way to find out what instructional strategies work best for them.

Keeping Students Inspired About Learning

I am fully aware that many urban and rural schools are considered high performing. These schools have dynamite principals, leadership teams, support teams, and classroom teachers who have nurtured a school culture in which failure is not an option; excellence is demanded of everyone in the building. Anything less than excellence is unacceptable in these high-performing schools. Some of these schools are in the heart of the most dangerous neighborhoods in the country. Within their walls is an oasis of hope and dreams; of purpose, mission, and vision;

of hard work, dedication, and commitment. These schools consistently show the world what urban and rural students can achieve when they are in the right school environment and with the right people leading and teaching.

Equally impressive are those urban and rural schools that are transforming their culture—perennially low-performing schools that are suddenly on the road to success. Excitement is in the air at these schools; teachers and leaders are fired up about coming to work every day and taking their teaching to the next level. Students are excited about the changes, too, and ready to put forth maximum effort. It's a new day in these schools, and everyone involved can smell victory in the air.

Unfortunately, the schools discussed above do not represent the majority, but rather a microscopic minority. Thousands upon thousands of children across the United States attend chronically low-performing schools where the climate and culture are so toxic that closing the attitude gap becomes almost impossible. The students here are not inspired to put forth maximum effort. They do not see the light at the end of the tunnel—how success in school translates into success in life beyond school.

This is where you come in. You are the authority of the room with your name on it. What will you do with this authority? How will you keep your students inspired about learning? How can you inspire them if you do not know them? How can you inspire them if *they* do not know *you*?

Keeping Students Motivated to Excel

Recently, I presented at a school in the Northeast about two weeks before summer vacation. It was an awkward time to conduct a professional development workshop, given that the teachers were winding down for the year, but it was clear that the teachers were dedicated and working hard up until the last day. During the question/answer period, a teacher expressed to me that she was tired and worn out and didn't feel she was connecting with her students. As she spoke, she began to cry. "Principal Kafele," she said to me, "how do *I* stay motivated over the course of 10 months while simultaneously keeping my students motivated?"

Although I could have shared many specific strategies with this teacher for motivating her students, I decided to challenge her to look within herself by conducting the self-reflection activity discussed in Chapter 2. I asked her, "In the context of your frustration with keeping your students motivated at the end of the year given your own year-end fatigue, *who are you?*" She answered by sharing all her positive attributes as a teacher. Then I asked her, "In the context of your frustration with keeping your students motivated at the end of the year and your own year-end fatigue, *what are you about?*" She answered by sharing her purpose for teaching. Finally, I asked her, "*What is your most recent evidence* confirming your answers to the previous two questions?" I challenged the teacher to "dig deep," and she did. She subsequently thanked me for the challenge; she said it was the motivation she needed to get through the final two weeks of the school year. She had the answer to her problem; she simply had not reflected deeply enough to locate it. This is the case for most of us: The answers that we're looking for are usually deep within us.

Knowing Your Students' Goals and Aspirations

Do your students have academic and personal goals for this school year? If so, do you know what they are? Are they written and posted? What are your students' long-range aspirations? Are they doing the things now that will make their aspirations a reality later? Do you see them intentionally preparing for their success?

Goal setting is a powerful concept, particularly for students in underperforming schools. Without concrete goals to aim for, students are essentially reduced to nothing but wanderers. They must be more than wanderers; they must be fervent pursuers of their goals and dreams. Too many students, living lives of day-to-day survival, do not dare to dream; it is essential that we as teachers encourage them to develop aspirations.

Many students find it hard to come up with concrete goals and aspirations because they simply do not know what's out there for them. They may have heard of particular professions—doctors, lawyers, teachers, police officers, firefighters—but even then, they have no idea what the professions entail. It is your job to gauge your students' awareness of the thousands of possible career paths out there. If we fail to help our students see the connection between what they learn in school and possible future careers, then our students are bound to underperform.

Again, relationships are the key here: You have to know your students, and you have to know what they know. They have to feel comfortable speaking to you openly and honestly about their goals and aspirations; if there is any sort of barrier between you and your students, then a true relationship will never develop. Open lines of communication are absolutely essential.

Knowing Your Students' Needs and Interests

In my 21 years as a teacher and a principal, I worked exclusively in urban school districts. The free and reduced-price lunch populations in my schools typically hovered between 85 and 90 percent, so most of my students came from economically disadvantaged households. However, my fellow educators were predominantly middle-class adults, meaning they brought the perspectives and assumptions of middle-class adults with them to school every day. In and of itself, this is not necessarily a bad thing; the problem occurs when teachers impose their assumptions on students without taking the students' backgrounds, including their needs and interests, into consideration.

Students' Needs

In addition to the three most basic survival needs—food, clothing, and shelter—your students have a wide variety of needs that must be met if they stand a chance to focus on maximizing their academic potential. If you have no relationship with your students, you will never know what their needs are. In many classrooms across the United States, there are children whose basic survival needs are either not being met or are being met at minimal levels—and their teachers are not even aware.

Tens of thousands of children report to school hungry every year because they have no food to eat at home. How and why do we expect these children to focus on learning complex subjects in class when they are sitting in their classrooms hungry? Although many schools serve free breakfast in the morning, many older students avoid it because they do not want their peers to know that their parents cannot afford to feed them at home. In addition to going hungry, many students are homeless and living in deplorable conditions—but again, if you have no relationship with your students, you will never know this. At best, you will know that your students are homeless, but you will not know the extent of their living conditions and its effect on their ability to learn in your classroom.

Beyond basic survival needs, children have a plethora of unmet but attainable needs that inhibit their ability to soar academically. For example, many children have a strong need to be accepted by their peers. This need is often immensely important to students, but without developing a relationship with them, you'll never know how much they're affected by it.

Students' Interests
As with needs, students have many interests that middle-class teachers may not know about. It is imperative that you learn

your students' interests—after all, interests can be turned into careers. When I conduct motivational assemblies at schools, I capture students' attention by helping them connect their interests to possible career paths. I tell them that there is no need for them to lead miserable work lives if they can find a way to turn their interests into careers or entrepreneurial ventures.

Knowing Your Students' Experiences and Realities

Do you know what it's like to walk in your students' shoes? Could you handle the experiences that your students deal with outside of school every day?

Because of the relationships I developed with my students, I knew what conditions they were going home to every day. I gathered this information not only through conversations but also through visits to students' homes. For example, I remember going to visit one of my 5th graders when I was her teacher. Upon entering the lobby of her apartment building, I saw gang members congregating in the stairwell, all clad in bandanas of the same color, and violent graffiti all over the walls. In order to get to the student's apartment, I had to walk past the gang members. I only had to "endure" this experience the handful of times that I visited the student, but for her it was an everyday reality. Could I endure it? Could *you* endure it? In any case, despite what I learned about the student's home life, I expected her to come to school each and every day ready to soar. There were no excuses.

Here's another example. One day, on a home visit to one of my 6th graders' apartment, the girl's mother asked me to stay for dinner. As we ate, I noticed two mice running around the living room. Neither the girl nor her mother had any reaction. Still, I expected this student to soar in class—no excuses.

One more example: When I worked as a principal, I once went to visit a student at his apartment because I could not reach his mother by phone. Upon my arrival, I was told that this boy lived on the 15th floor and that the elevator didn't work—a common situation in this particular building. Walking through a stairwell that reeked of urine and garbage all the way up to the 15th floor was a brutal experience, to say the least. Though I now understood a bit more about this student's reality, once again, I refused to use it as an excuse; as with the other two students, I expected this student to soar.

Knowing Your Students' Challenges and Obstacles

What kind of unique challenges do your students face? How do these challenges affect their desire to excel in your classroom? Can these challenges be overcome? Are you in a position to help them to overcome these challenges?

One of my first rude awakenings when I became a principal was discovering the number of high-performing students I had who couldn't afford to attend a 4-year college. Though some of these students received partial scholarships, they still couldn't afford to pay the balance of their tuition. Unfortunately, students have to play the hand they're dealt. Although excuses are not acceptable, the reality is that many students will continue to encounter challenges that their more affluent counterparts may not have to face. As a teacher, you must be familiar with your students' unique challenges.

Knowing Your Students' Parents

The involvement and engagement of parents in their students' education is essential to ensure academic achievement. Students whose parents believe that education is the key to their children's success are far more likely to do well in school than those whose parents are uninvolved and disengaged. If you do not know your student's parents, you do not fully know your students. When I mention this at workshops, many teachers reply to me that it can be virtually impossible to get to know some of their students' parents. I remind them that reaching out to parents does not and should not be solely an individual endeavor, but rather must be the whole school community's responsibility. School staff must work collaboratively to devise strategies that will work to get parents involved. When parental engagement is a building-level priority—perhaps even folded into the overall mission of the school—students ultimately benefit.

Knowing Your Students' Neighborhoods

Do you know your students' neighborhoods? Do you understand their neighborhoods? Do you respect their neighborhoods?

I remind teachers all the time that they must be careful when they talk about their students' neighborhoods because students often *are* their neighborhoods—they are the products of their unique surroundings. When you lack knowledge of your students' neighborhoods, you lack knowledge of your students. When you lack an understanding of your students' neighborhoods, you lack an understanding of your students. When you lack respect for your students' neighborhoods, you lack respect for your students.

So, get to know your students' neighborhoods. This doesn't mean you have to be a fixture on their streets, but it does mean that you need to develop some level of familiarity that goes well beyond stereotypes and generalizations.

4 Compassion for Students
Do I Care About Them?

REFLECTIVE QUESTIONS

Before reading this chapter, look into a mirror and ask yourself the following questions about your students:

1. Do they perceive that I care about them?

2. Do they perceive that I like them?

3. Do they perceive that I appreciate them?

4. Do they perceive that I respect them?

5. Do they perceive that I understand them?

6. Do they perceive that I have empathy toward them?

7. Do they perceive that I am patient with them?

8. Do they perceive that I treat them equally and fairly?

9. Do they perceive that I am committed to them?

10. Do they perceive that I fear them?

As of this writing, my youngest son, Jabari, is a sophomore in college. It is more than evident that he likes his school. When he talks to me about his classes there, what stands out most for me is the genuine compassion that so many of the professors seem to have for him and his peers. Several of Jabari's professors have told him that they appreciate him and that they feel that he will go far in life. This feedback has had a very positive effect on Jabari's self-image. By contrast, in high school, Jabari's teachers may have had the same level of compassion, but he was not aware of it; nobody told him how they felt about him.

I believe strongly that the importance of expressing compassion for students is given far too little attention by the education community. Students must feel and know that their teachers care about them if they are to succeed. As with the other strands in this book, developing compassion for students requires building a relationship with them. (The reverse is true as well: Relationships without compassion are like plants without water—they won't last very long.) Your students must know that they have a teacher who truly cares about them, who is in their corner, and who does not believe that quitting on them is ever an option.

Showing Students That You Care About Them

In my professional development workshops, I usually ask the assembled educators to raise their hand if they care about their students. Obviously, all hands go up. I then proceed to explore the question of perception. I remind my audience that we can *claim* to care about our students all we want, but the true test is whether or not they *perceive* that we care. Students work hard and give their best when they know that their teachers care about them and their progress, because they are motivated to make their teachers proud.

Whenever I speak with students in small groups, I like to ask them whether or not they feel that their teachers care about them. It is astounding how many students respond that they do not feel that their teachers care about them. It is always painful to hear from so many students who do not feel that their teachers are in their corner, regardless of how accurate their perceptions are.

Showing Students That You Like Them

Do you like your students? Do you like all of them? Are there any students in your classroom you don't particularly like?

I am frequently asked if I believe that nonblack teachers can effectively teach black students. Though I used to harbor doubts, my years of teaching and leading have made it perfectly clear to me that a teacher's race or ethnicity is not the issue. Effective teachers must, above all, like children—*all* children.

Children know when they are not liked; it is blatantly obvious to them. Or so they think: Teachers may in fact like a given student very much, but the student's perception is different, and perception is what matters.

You must pay particular attention to the way your students react to you. You must gauge their perceptions of whether or not you like them. Students formulate an opinion as to whether or not you like them based on how you treat them in the classroom. Do you demonstrate your appreciation for them? Your actual interactions communicate more than your intended meaning. What you say and how you say it lets your students know exactly how you feel about them.

Showing Students That You Appreciate Them

Each of your students brings to the classroom his or her own special and unique characteristics, talents, and challenges. Each student is different, but all of them are special. They all have the capacity to maximize their potential, based in large part on your ability to make solid connections with them. One way to do this is by showing students that you appreciate them. This is very easy to do with students who have ideal home lives and are already self-motivated, but what about the students whose challenges outside of school manifest themselves in the classroom? What about the students who come to school feeling unappreciated? You must pay particular attention to these students and show them through your interactions that you appreciate them for the work they do in the classroom as well as simply for being who they are.

If there happens to be a student who poses a particular challenge for you, it is incumbent upon you to identify his good qualities and exploit them. You want to find excuses for letting the student know that you appreciate him. Chances are that he hears more than enough criticism about his poor grades or behavior; he doesn't need more of the same from you. Your role is to counter your criticisms of his negative behaviors with expressions of appreciation toward him. Speak to him in a way that makes him feel good about himself so that he begins to feel that his inappropriateness has no place in your classroom. Speak to him in a way that allows him to develop trust in his relationship with you and to know that he always has your support. Remember, what's key here is *attitude transformation*— closing the attitude gap in your classroom.

Showing Students That You Respect Them

A few years ago, a newly hired teacher on my staff was really struggling with his students. Nothing he did seemed to work for him; the students were consistently disruptive every day. When I visited his classroom, it was clear to me that the issue was one of respect. It appeared to me that these students didn't feel respected by their teacher, so they, in turn, did not respect him. One day, the teacher was absent, so I spent some time in the classroom speaking with the students. I asked them how they perceived the problem in their classroom. As I suspected, they indicated that their new teacher did not respect them, and that this was why they behaved the way they did.

Although we are the authority figures in our classrooms, we must still be very much mindful of our interactions with our students. Anytime you shout at students, for example, you run the risk of alienating them and making them feel as though you don't respect them. Students want to feel respected, particularly by you in the presence of their peers; it is important for many of them to "save face" in front of classmates. Here's an example. An administrator recently shared with me that she yelled at a student to throw his tray in the garbage during lunchtime in the cafeteria. The student refused, and a showdown ensued—purely because, in the student's eyes, the administrator hadn't shown him respect. If, however, the administrator had considered the importance of perceived respect to the student, he could have approached him in a non-offensive way (e.g., by going directly to the student rather than shouting across the cafeteria) and avoided a confrontation.

Again: *It is not what we say, it is what they perceive.* In your interactions with students, you must demonstrate your respect for them through what you say and how you say it.

Showing Students That You Understand Them

During my professional development workshops, I remind my audiences of some of the realities of growing up in urban environments. I remind them that life in the inner city is not some television drama that resolves itself in an hour. This is *real*—this is students' *lives*. There's no switch that the students can turn on and off.

There's an organization in a city not far from where I live that stages a weekly protest rally every Wednesday afternoon. There have been 158 consecutive weekly protests over the past three years. Their purpose is to protest violence and murders in the city. Every week, the organization holds its protest at an intersection in the city where a murder or shooting recently occurred. There's never been a problem locating an intersection.

This is the reality of the students in so many urban centers throughout the United States. This is their truth; it shapes who they are, how they think, and what they bring to the classroom every day. Do you understand your students' reality? Do they perceive that you understand them?

When educators tell me how angry some of their students are, I remind them that some of their students return to neighborhoods and homes that they themselves could never imagine enduring. Of course they are angry! Who wouldn't be? Imagine what happens when angry children come into a classroom led by a teacher who doesn't understand the extent of their anger or where the anger is coming from. This is a highly combustible situation. Your role is to make your classroom an oasis where students can temporarily remove themselves from their outside realities—where they can focus on their education so they can one day permanently escape those realities. You have to demonstrate to your students that despite the obstacles they may face every day, and despite the challenges that these obstacles pose for you and your mission as a teacher, you genuinely understand what they are dealing with inside and outside of school on a regular basis.

Showing Students That You Empathize with Them

Empathy is closely associated with understanding. The life challenges that so many children face in their daily lives simply cannot be ignored. It affects not only their ability to learn and to be successful in your classroom, but also their desire to even want to do so.

I recall as a classroom teacher taking my students' "stories" home with me regularly. I couldn't leave them at the job; they stayed with me 24/7. I remember many days sitting at my desk in my classroom after hours, literally weeping over my students' stories. For example, when I taught 5th grade, one of my high-performing male students was accosted and beaten up by several older boys on his walk home from school. This upset me to no end. Upon hearing about the assault, I sat at my desk and wept for both him and his mother.

There's a fine line between empathy and sympathy. I made a decision early on in my teaching mission that I could not and would not feel sorry for my students. I knew that my sympathy was not going to help my students maximize their potential; my empathy, however, was essential. My students needed me to understand, identify with, and relate to them, not to feel sorry for them. They needed me to know about their plight, but also to push them hard so that they may successfully overcome it. They also needed me to listen to them, because they needed to be heard. As Hart & Kindle Hodson (2004) note, "If we want our students to think for themselves, to be honest and authentic, we need to be reflective, honest, and authentic ourselves. If we want our students to know that their thoughts and feelings matter to us, we will take the time to listen to them and to consider their points of view" (p. 25).

It is imperative that you, too, have empathy for your students. They don't need you to feel sorry for them; they simply need you to understand them and to use that understanding to push them to previously unimagined heights.

Showing Students That You're Patient with Them

In today's times of high-stakes testing, there are enormous pressures on teachers and students to perform. With such intense pressure, it becomes very easy to lose sight of the fundamental purpose of education: *to learn.* If your students are going to perform well on standardized assessments as well as strive for excellence in all of their educational endeavors, you must demonstrate patience with them throughout the process. Because students do not all learn alike, think alike, or behave alike, it is vital that you appreciate their differences and demonstrate patience with them all. Your students are not all going to achieve success at the same time, and any failure to demonstrate patience can discourage those who learn at a slower pace—and discouragement translates into low performance.

Showing Students That You Treat Them Equally and Fairly

How do you treat your students? Do you treat them equally? Do you treat them fairly? How do your students perceive your treatment of them?

You simply cannot get the most out of your students if they perceive that you treat them unequally and unfairly. They want to feel valued. They want to feel appreciated. They want to feel respected. When differential treatment exists, resentment sets in among students, leading to unnecessary tension in a classroom. To avoid this, take action to ensure that your students perceive you as treating them all in a fair and equal manner.

Showing Students That You're Committed to Them

After all is said and done, your students have to be convinced that you are committed to their educational growth and development. They have to feel and perceive that your purpose for reporting to work every day is to help them soar. They have to know that you are there for them.

I have been in many classrooms over the years where it was apparent that the teacher was not committed to the students—you could sense it in the lack of respect demonstrated on both sides of teacher-student interactions. You could also sense it in the teacher's low standards and expectations for students.

A few years back, when I was working as a principal, a local television show did a story on me. I was not aware that the story was being done, so I had no influence in its outcome. As a part of the story, the show's producers interviewed some of my students. One of my students said something that I've since reflected upon often. He said, "Mr. Kafele really cares about us. He even buys us lunch when we have no lunch money to pay for it." Although the student used the word "care," he was essentially saying that I was committed to him and his class-mates—which I was.

You, too, must demonstrate an obvious commitment to your students' overall educational growth and development. You must consistently demonstrate to them that they matter, that they are important, and that you will do whatever it takes to ensure their success, no matter the challenges.

Showing Students That You Don't Fear Them

Do you fear any of your students? Do they perceive that you fear them?

I will never forget an experience I had at a school a few years back, when I was working as a consultant. The principal and I were walking down a crowded hallway during class time at an urban high school when a male student walked in our direc-tion. The young man had a hat on, his pants were sagging, and he was deeply engrossed in a cellphone conversation. I won-dered how the principal was going to handle both the young man and the crowded hallway during instructional time. The young man simply walked right past us as if we weren't there. When I asked the principal if he was going to address the student's behavior, he responded that it was typical and too far out of control to correct.

I could not believe what I was hearing, but I understood it. Clearly, there were some climate and culture issues at this school. It was obvious to me that fear was in the air—the principal was too afraid to address either the student on the phone or the other students in the hallway.

We can't motivate, educate, and empower students if we fear them. We can't transform attitudes if we fear them, either. Once students perceive that their teachers fear them, making positive connections with them becomes virtually impossible. You cannot fear any student in your classroom. Demonstrating a fear of your students completely undermines your authority as the teacher and renders you incapable of closing the attitude gap within your classroom. From day one, you must establish your authority as the teacher. You can't effectively teach and inspire if you are not perceived as the respected authority figure in your classroom.

5 | Environment for Learning
Do I Provide My Students with an Environment of Excellence?

REFLECTIVE QUESTIONS

Before reading this chapter, look into a mirror and ask yourself the following questions about your students:

1. Do I provide them with a learning environment of excellence?

2. Do I have our classroom mission and vision statements posted?

3. Do I have our building-level standardized assessment objectives posted?

4. Do I have our classroom academic excellence criteria posted?

5. Do I have our student goals and strategies posted?

6. Do I have a "Wall of Fame" posted?

7. Do I have motivational quotes and affirmations posted?

8. Do I have historical images that reflect my students posted?

9. Do I have the names and pictures of colleges and universities posted?

10. Do I have the names of careers and their descriptions posted?

When I taught 5th grade, the district decided to departmentalize all subject areas. Each teacher was to teach one subject area, and I opted to teach Social Studies. To prepare my students for success in my classroom, I decided to create a learning environment that spoke not only to the subject area but also to motivating my students. I designated a different area of the classroom walls for each of the following items:

- A list of subject-area "students of the week"
- A list of homework "students of the week"
- A list of attendance "students of the week"
- Goal-setting charts
- Student work samples

Throughout the classroom, I also posted signs and posters of colleges and universities; motivational quotes and affirmations; the classroom mission and vision statements; historical images that reflected my students' backgrounds; the names and descriptions of different careers and occupations; our school's criteria for academic excellence, including behavioral expectations; and our standardized-assessment goals. The environment that I created for my students was stimulating and engaging.

I used my classroom walls to create a classroom climate and culture that shaped my students' attitudes.

Around midyear, our principal called all of the 5th grade teachers together for a meeting after school. I remember it like it was yesterday. She said that the movement of students between classes was too loud, so effective immediately, the teachers would move from class to class instead. I could not believe what I was hearing—I knew that a large part of my students' success, not to mention my own, was due to the learning environment that I had created. Teaching my students in someone else's learning environment would be less than optimal; in some of the classrooms there was absolutely nothing on the walls.

I anxiously expressed my concerns to the principal. "I need my own learning environment in order to be effective," I said. "My walls play a large part in transforming my students' attitudes." She looked at me and replied, "Kafele, I suggest you strap your learning environment on your back and take it along with you to each classroom!" I will never forget those words. I proceeded to passionately explain the significance of my classroom learning environment. I told her that we would ensure that the halls were quiet between classes. She conceded, and the teachers stayed in their classrooms.

When I became a principal, I retained my conviction that students shouldn't come into a school with bare walls. I had to ensure that the entire school's wall space was utilized the same way I utilized my classroom wall space. The items on those walls, both in the classrooms and throughout the school, played a major role in shaping the overall learning environment that I felt my students required in order to be successful. Those walls changed our students' attitudes; those walls welcomed our students to school. Fisher, Frey, and Pumpian (2012) ask, "Can our school be so welcoming, so inviting, and so comfortable that every person who walks through our doors believes they are about to have an amazing experience? Quite simply, can our stakeholders (that is, our visitors, vendors, parents, staff, and students) feel welcomed? There must be one simple answer to these questions, and that is an emphatic yes!" (p. 17). I am in full agreement. The classroom environment that you create for your students is crucial for closing the attitude gap and achievement gap. True learning cannot begin until the environment dictates that it is okay to learn.

A few years ago, when I first began addressing the environment for learning in my workshops, I worried that veteran teachers may feel that they didn't need to hear about it—that it was too elementary a topic. When I eventually went on the road as a full-time consultant, I became convinced that the topic needed to be addressed. As I visited classrooms, I noticed that many of the things I expected to see were simply not present.

Providing Students with a Learning Environment of Excellence

What does your classroom learning environment look like? Does it encourage your students to strive to achieve excellence? Does it encourage them to maximize their potential? Does it make your students want to return to it every day? Is it neat?

Is it clean? Is it organized? Is it well stocked with books and other reading material?

I always say that the classroom learning environment must communicate to students, "Come on in! This is the place to be!" I have seen classrooms across the country at the elementary, middle, and high school levels that do just that—they are vibrant, stimulating, and engaging. Such an environment plays a powerful role toward closing the attitude gap, enabling students to learn at the highest levels.

As a child, until I moved to central New Jersey when I was in high school, all I knew was the inner city; it was my world. Ever since I started speaking nationally in 2004, I've made it a priority to visit the neighborhoods of the cities where I speak. I want to see the neighborhoods in which the students live— especially the economically disadvantaged ones. I want to see their homes, their buildings, their shops; I want to see what the kids are doing outside of school hours. I am always curious as to what alternatives to hanging out in the streets exist for students in different cities.

What I've seen is typical of inner-city neighborhoods in the United States: decadence, decay, and urban blight. You can drive through some of these neighborhoods and see houses with bars on their windows everywhere—families essentially rendered prisoners in their own homes. In many of these neighborhoods, residents are afraid to leave their homes due to the proliferation of gangs and violence.

Of course, as I've noted previously, poor living conditions are
no excuse for the children of these disadvantaged neighborhoods not to attend school each and every day, ready to excel.
Your role is to create an alternative environment for students—
a special environment of hope and promise, one that makes
a sad child happy and an isolated child feel special, one that
makes a child with low self-esteem feel as though she can
become the president of the United States if she works hard
and applies herself.

A learning environment of excellence is neat, clean, and
organized throughout the course of the day. We know that the
evening custodians are going to have the classrooms prepared
for homeroom, but what about afternoon classes? Will the
rooms be just as orderly for students then as they were at the
start of the day? I cannot overstate the importance of neatness,
cleanliness, and organization for motivating students in the
classroom.

Posting the Classroom Mission and Vision Statements

When I walk onto a school campus, the first thing I look for is
how clean the outside grounds and front lobby are. I also focus
on how I'm being greeted as I enter the building, and by whom.
My next priority is to identify the posted school mission and
vision statements. I don't want to see anything else until I
have seen these statements, preferably posted in the lobby. The
school mission statement will tell me what the school *is* and
what it is *about*; it will give me a sense of the school's identity

and reveal its purpose for being. The school vision statement will tell me where the school is going. It will give me a sense of where stakeholders believe the school needs to be and how much progress it has made over a period of time. All staff and students should know both the mission and vision statements and be required to recite them daily (during the morning announcements, for example). Classrooms ought to post mission and vision statements of their own as well, particularly at the elementary and middle school levels. Each classroom has its own unique characteristics that its mission and vision statements should address while remaining consistent with the overall school mission and vision statements.

In your own classroom, do you have mission and vision statements? Are they posted? Are they visible? Are students required to recite them daily? Were students given an opportunity to offer their own input into the development of your classroom mission and vision statements, thus giving them a greater sense of ownership and empowerment?

Classroom mission and vision statements should be no more than two sentences long and posted in a highly visible location of your classroom so that all of your students can see them. When I walk into a school and see paragraph-long mission and vision statements, I know that the chances that they have been memorized and recited daily are slim to none. These statements should be concise yet powerful, so that the point of each is clearly made.

Posting Building-Level Standardized Assessment Objectives

When I ask educators at all levels what the current adequate yearly progress (AYP) benchmark is, most of them know; when I ask students, most of them don't. I have never understood this: How can you expect students to do their best as a school community if they don't have a target to aim for? The AYP is the target; it's the goal. How can you reach a goal if it's never been set?

In my first year as the principal of a middle school in New Jersey, I realized that my students had no clue about the district objectives for standardized assessments. I knew that there was no way that we were going to perform at optimal levels if they had no target to aim for. I had to get my students to see themselves as a community—a family of learners; I wanted them to approach their standardized assessments not solely as individuals but as a school, and I wanted them to do it with the right attitude: *We are a great school, and we can perform with the best of them.*

The first week of school, I convened the entire student body and staff in the auditorium and used bar graphs to show them how our performance compared to schools in wealthier neighborhoods. The students couldn't believe how much better the wealthier schools were doing. I asked them if they were willing to accept this as their reality. In unison, they shouted back, "No!" I then told them the AYP benchmark for that year, and that we would reach it or surpass it. They agreed, and we went to work.

I posted the AYP benchmark in every classroom, in the hallways, in the cafeteria, and even in the bathrooms. I spoke about them over the PA every day. I needed my students to see and hear the goal every day and ultimately internalize it. At the same time, I had to ensure that students didn't start to think that the purpose of attending school was to pass a standardized test.

In my third year at the school, we finally met the AYP benchmark that I'd posted all over the building. Students and staff were elated. Changing student attitudes by giving them concrete goals made the difference. I strongly encourage you to do the same with your students: Change their mindsets so that they approach state standardized assessments collectively—as "we" rather than "me."

Posting Criteria for Academic Excellence

I have asked students over the years, "What does it mean to be excellent in your school?" Although the very generic answers that the students typically provide are acceptable, they do not speak to the specific expectations of their teachers or school. There is so much that students must know that we too often take for granted. If we want students to perform at the highest levels of proficiency, we must actually explain to them exactly what that is. At a minimum, your criteria for academic excellence should be comprised of the following: academic expectations, homework expectations, and behavioral expectations.

Academic Expectations

It is my long-held belief that all students should be held accountable for striving to achieve academic distinction (e.g., honor roll, honorable mention) every marking period. Do your students know the criteria for achieving academic distinction? Are the criteria spelled out somewhere to which students can refer? In many of the schools I have visited over the years, only a minority of the student population meets the criteria for academic distinction, but it doesn't have to be this way. It's all about changing attitudes by keeping students informed. To that end, be sure to post the criteria for academic distinction and refer to them frequently. Students have to know exactly what excellence is considered to be in your classroom if they are going to strive to attain it.

Homework Expectations

It is simply not enough to tell students and their parents that homework is due the day after it is assigned. Your approach must be much more systematic. Your students have to understand that while homework is important as a way to reinforce the day's lesson, it is also important because it reflects the high expectations that you have set in your classroom. Be sure to post your expectations for homework completion. Here are a few possible criteria:

- Writing on the front side of the paper only
- Black or dark blue ink only (except in math, where a pencil is required)
- Cursive handwriting on all non-math–related assignments

- Proper headings
- No folded work
- No wrinkled work
- No torn work
- No smudges or smears
- Minimal grammatical errors
- Due the following day unless otherwise noted

Putting your homework policy in writing and posting it on
your classroom wall once again reinforces the expectations that
you have for your students and helps set the tone of the learning environment. It also serves as a mirror of sorts, remind-
ing students that the quality of the work that they submit is a
reflection of who they are.

Behavioral Expectations

To close the attitude gap and achieve high academic performance in your classroom, it is essential that your students
internalize your behavioral expectations—not rules, but expectations. Rules define what students can and cannot do in your
classroom; expectations, by contrast, speak to the standards
you have set for your students' behavior. Rules do not change
attitudes; expectations do. The best way to ensure that students
know how you expect them to behave is to post your expectations in a visible area and discuss them with your students
regularly. You must also hold your students accountable for
meeting your expectations, or else the words that you post will
serve little purpose beyond wall decoration.

Posting Student Goals and Strategies

Now here's a topic that I am absolutely passionate about. Whenever I met with my staff in my days as a principal, I would invariably find an excuse to bring up goal setting. I would frequently remind my staff that goal setting works when implemented in earnest; the problem is that so few of us understand the true power of setting concrete goals and devising strategies to achieve them.

During my professional development workshops, I ask educators to raise their hands if they require their students to set academic goals for a given marking period, write a strategy for how they will achieve their goals (both at home and in school), and post both the goals and the strategy on the classroom wall. Not a lot of hands usually go up, so I challenge the teachers: "Are you telling me that you expect excellence from your students but you don't require them to set goals in order to achieve it? If students don't have targets to aim for, they are essentially just wandering aimlessly throughout the day, every day."

Your objective is to close the attitude gap and, eventually, the achievement gap. The climate and culture of your school and classroom must encourage your students to put forth maximum effort to be successful. One way to do this is to teach students how to set specific goals and devise a plan to achieve them. As Jackson (2011) notes, "Goal setting and tracking progress toward those goals makes the idea of successful investment more tangible" (p. 88).

Creating a Goal Chart

Unwritten goals are essentially dreams that can be easily forgotten. Goals must be made concrete by writing them down. I suggest creating a "goal chart"—a sheet of paper on which students write their goals for the marking period along with the strategies they intend to use to meet them (see figure).

Sample Goal Chart

Goal Chart for 1st Marking Period

Name: _____

Current Standing
Language Arts:	A
Math:	A
Science:	C
Social Studies:	B

Goals
Language Arts:	A
Math:	A
Science:	B
Social Studies:	A

Strategy

Language Arts (In Class): _____

Language Arts (At Home): _____

Math (In Class): _____

Math (At Home): _____

Science (In Class): _____

Science (At Home): _____

Social Studies (In Class): _____

Social Studies (At Home): _____

Goal Chart Section 1: Current Standing. The first part of the goal chart answers the question "Where am I now?" Students must assess where they currently stand academically and write it down in the "Current Standing" section of the goal chart. This becomes the starting point—the base—for the rest of the process. Beneath the Current Standing section, each of the subjects that your students are currently taking in your classroom should be listed. (If yours is a departmentalized classroom, then the subject being taught would be written here.) Next to each subject, the student's current grade should be entered. (If you are at the start of the first marking period and no grades have been assigned yet, assume an *A* for each subject.) If you don't want your students' current grades to be made public, simply skip the Current Standing section and proceed to part two: goals.

Goal Chart Section 2: Goals. This part of the goal chart answers the question "Where am I going?" In this section, along the left-hand margin, students list the same subject areas as in the Current Standing section along with the grade that they project they will achieve in each during the marking period. The goals that your students set for each marking period should be

- **Challenging**—Unless students are already getting an *A* in a given subject, they should be striving to improve on the grades listed in the Current Standing section.
- **Realistic**—If a student currently has an *F* in math, a goal of getting an *A* is probably unrealistic, as the student likely needs to brush up on some foundational

skills. The whole idea is to set the student up for success rather than failure.

- **Attainable**—Achieving a goal is an accomplishment and therefore an incentive to do even better the next marking period. If goals are not within reach, however, students are deprived of the opportunity to experience this short-term accomplishment that is also a stepping-stone to long-range success.

Strategy

Developing a strategy is the hardest part of the goal-setting process. This is when you actually devise and compose a plan of action for achieving your goals. Your plan of action asks the question "How will I get there?" I always recommend a two-part plan for each subject area, one for school and one for home: Your students will write a plan outlining what they need to do *in class* in order to be successful and, separately, what they need to do *at home* in order to be successful. At the elementary and middle school levels, it is important that you help your students devise and compose a strategy.

Once your students' goal charts are fully completed, they should be posted in a section of the classroom that is designated for them. If your classroom is self-contained, your students should draft their charts on notebook paper or type them up; if classes are departmentalized, then an index card will suffice for the subject that you teach. Some teachers I have worked with over the years have turned goal charts into elaborate artistic projects, enabling students to take greater ownership of them by personalizing them (for example, by including drawings or photos of themselves in their charts).

At the conclusion of the marking period, your students should be given the opportunity to compare their actual grades with the goals on their charts, followed up by a whole-class discussion or one-on-one conference with you to discuss next steps. Goal charts for the new marking period should be taped right over the previous chart so that ongoing comparisons can be made.

Posting a Wall of Fame

I am a big sports fan and typically make several sports analogies in my presentations. There is so much in sports that is applicable to what happens in classrooms every day. For example, in sports, both fans and athletes celebrate after a big play is run or a point is scored, even when a team is losing the game. The same should occur in the classroom: Educators must find the smallest excuses to celebrate their students' accomplishments. Too many students simply never hear praise directed at them; they hear the criticisms, condemnations, and putdowns, but hardly ever hear someone say, "Excellent!" or "Great job!" or "You are brilliant!" When children are told consistently that they are doing things well, they are more likely to continue what they're doing. If, however, they become accustomed to a steady stream of criticism, they're not as likely to change what they're doing because they've come to expect the criticism.

One way of celebrating your students on an ongoing basis is by posting a "Wall of Fame" in your classroom, the sole purpose of which is to celebrate your students' academic accomplishments (Reeves, 2004). This is your students' wall; it is all about them. There are obviously many categories of student achievement, but I will concentrate here on the following five types of recognition suitable for a Wall of Fame:

- Students who have been selected for the honor roll
- Subject area "students of the month"
- Homework "students of the month"
- Attendance "students of the month"
- Samples of outstanding student work

Of course, you can add other items and even acknowledge your students as frequently as you deem beneficial and appropriate. The bottom line is that you want to ensure that your classroom environment is student centered and that celebrating your students' accomplishments is of paramount importance.

Honor Roll

Most schools post their honor roll on a wall on the first floor. I am in full agreement with this initiative. The school's honor roll should be prominently displayed. I also believe strongly that the names of students who have made the honor roll should be displayed in those students' classrooms; such recognition gives them a sense of pride in their accomplishments and serves as an incentive for students who aren't on the honor roll.

Subject Area "Students of the Month"

When I was a first-year principal, I reviewed my school's existing "student of the month" program. The program typically acknowledged a very small number of students who were practically competing against each other, so I decided to expand it by including the top students in each subject area. These students wouldn't be competing against each other; they would simply have to meet the criteria I developed for recognition in each subject area. This way, a student who performs poorly in all subject areas but one might still find a way to be celebrated, which in turn might inspire her to strive for excellence in other subjects as well. There was no limit to the number of students who could be recognized as a subject area "student of the month."

I am recommending the same for you and your students. Develop criteria that are challenging but attainable. Here are some examples:

- Receives *A*s or *B*s on all tests and quizzes
- Receives *A*s or *B*s on all classroom projects
- Completes all homework assignments fully
- Displays excellent classroom behavior
- Participates extensively in class

Encourage your students to strive to meet the criteria every month. At the end of each month, post certificates or lists of all of the students who have met the criteria on a section of your Wall of Fame. My students loved seeing their names posted on the Wall of Fame—they would literally stand and stare at their names up there in awe.

Homework "Students of the Month"
On another section of the Wall of Fame, post certificates or a list of all students by subject area who completed all of their homework assignments in the previous month while also

adhering to the classroom homework policy. Such recognition is an incentive for all students to complete all homework assignments every month.

Attendance "Students of the Month"

Another section of your Wall of Fame could be reserved for recognizing attendance "students of the month." Here you might post certificates or a list of all students who attended school every day in the past month.

Samples of Outstanding Student Work

As a consultant, one of the first things that I look for when I enter a classroom is a selection of student work samples. The presence of student work on the walls sends a message to the students that the classroom is all about them, and that what they learn is so important that it needs to be displayed for everyone to see.

Once I locate posted student work samples in a classroom, the first thing I look for are the dates on the work. I want to see that the work is current; it disappoints me to see work that is more than a month old. When the samples are continuously updated, students are likelier to strive to do superior work, knowing that it might end up displayed on the wall.

Ceremony

On the first day of each month, you should lead your students in a short, informal ceremony at some designated time of the day, perhaps at the start or end of class. Use this ceremony to recognize students who met your criteria for having their names or works displayed on the Wall of Fame. This ceremony sends a message to all of your students that you value them, you value their work, and you value their academic growth and development. It works best when you put a lot of energy and enthusiasm into the ceremony, demonstrating to your students that you are proud of them and encouraging those who didn't make the Wall of Fame this time to work harder in the new month.

Again, there are many students sitting in your classroom who are unaccustomed to praise and recognition. They will go days without hearing someone say anything nice or positive about them. You must find every excuse imaginable to make your students feel good about themselves. Depending on your time and situation, you might even choose to recognize students on a weekly rather than a monthly basis; this is entirely up to you.

Posting Motivational Quotes and Affirmations

I recommend typing up motivational quotes and affirmations in large print on colored letter-sized paper and displaying them throughout the classroom. In my 2009 book *Motivating Black Males to Achieve in School and in Life,* I included a list of 50 affirmations that I refer to as "Principal Kafele's 50 *I*s for Being a Serious Student." Here are five of them:

- I believe in myself and in my ability to achieve academic excellence.
- I have a definite purpose for receiving an education.
- I understand my obligation to excel.

- I am determined to achieve academic excellence.
- I have a vision for achieving academic excellence.

When I was a teacher, to keep the classroom surroundings positive, I would post several of these affirmations on the walls and refer to them frequently throughout the course of each school year. I wanted my students to internalize each message. Later, when I became a principal, I went a step further: I placed all 50 affirmations on separate signs and posted them throughout the entire school, on all floors of the building. I also used the halls as my own personal classroom, bringing students over to any given affirmation between classes and using it as a teaching tool. It was all about creating a positive environment to develop positive students.

Posting Historical Images That Reflect Your Students

The achievement gap between high-achieving white and Asian students and low-achieving black and Latino students shows no real signs of closing any time soon. I have argued for years that this is due to a lack of emphasis on the attitude of the students. Until we begin to pay close attention to student attitudes in earnest, we will continue to see a wide gap in achievement.

As educators, we must focus our attention on the models, examples, and images of success that young people, particularly those in urban and rural districts, have before them. Far too many young people locate, identify with, and gravitate toward negative role models—and you are in a position to provide them with alternatives.

Here we are in the new millennium, and the media continue to bombard us with black and Latino imagery that is negative, destructive, or comedic. Through the lessons you teach, you can counter what your students see in the media by broadening their exposure—which may require you to broaden your own exposure as well (more on this in Chapter 6). Have you posted positive images in your classroom that reflect the ethnic composition of your students? What type of images do you have posted? What relevance do they have for your students? I encourage you to take these questions into consideration as you develop a classroom learning environment conducive to closing the attitude gap in your classroom.

Posting Names and Pictures of Colleges and Universities

It is never too early to encourage your students to start thinking about college; in fact, teachers should start doing so at the very beginning, in prekindergarten. To enhance such discussions, it's a good idea to hang posters on the wall that feature the names and pictures of colleges and universities. Many students come from households without any college graduates, so it's up to you as the teacher to make the prospect of higher education real. It is also a good idea to invite college graduates to your classroom to speak with your students and to take your students on field trips to college campuses.

Posting the Names and Descriptions of Careers

So many students are unaware of the endless possibilities that await them. I say to educators so often, "How can you expect your students to have diverse aspirations if they have not been exposed to the diverse opportunities that are out there for them?" There is so much that students of any background can aspire to—but without access to information about it, they cannot even conceptualize the possibilities.

I recommend that you identify space on your classroom walls to post a list of careers and their descriptions. Discuss these with your students, but also give them opportunities to read them on their own. The keys here are exposure and awareness: As these increase, students' attitudes about themselves and their prospects change for the better.

6 Relevance in Instruction

*Do I Realize Who
My Students Are?*

REFLECTIVE QUESTIONS

Before reading this chapter, look into a mirror and ask yourself the following questions about your students:

1. Do I realize who my students are?
2. Do my students realize who they are?
3. Do I think it's important for my students to learn "their story"?
4. Do my students think it's important to learn "their story"?
5. Do I have a responsibility to teach my students "their story"?
6. Do my students have a responsibility to learn "their story"?
7. Do my lessons take "their story" into consideration?
8. Do my students identify with and relate to what I teach them?
9. Will knowing "their story" affect the way my students see themselves?
10. Will knowing "their story" affect the way I see my students?

In Chapter 2, I mentioned how much I had looked forward to visiting Montgomery, Alabama, as a speaker. Another city I had been looking forward to visiting was Little Rock, Arkansas. For years, I had wanted to visit Little Rock Central High School, where nine black students (known as the "Little Rock Nine") were denied admission in 1957, three years following the U.S. Supreme Court's ruling outlawing forced segregation. The case of the Little Rock Nine was a pivotal event of the American Civil Rights Movement, and studying its history played a major role in my own transformation into the man and educator I am today. I read the story of the Little Rock Nine countless times; I admired them and was fascinated by their courage, and have always wondered if I could have endured what they endured. My invitation to visit Little Rock Central finally came in July 2010, when the school's principal e-mailed me to request that I conduct a professional development workshop for her staff. I was finally going to see the inside of this historic building.

In learning about the Little Rock Nine and other aspects of African American history, I was simultaneously learning about myself. I was connecting with the totality of African American history—I saw it as being me, and me as being it. I saw myself as a descendant of a people who achieved and endured much over the centuries, but I also saw myself as a part of a continuum: I grew to understand that my role was to continue this great legacy. This is the reason I do what I have been doing the past 24 years. My mission as an educator is a direct result of what I learned, including my exposure to the Little Rock Nine and other stories in African American history. These stories were most relevant for me and helped me to better understand the rest of the world. By reading about the greatness of African Americans who came before me, I began to view myself differently; seeing myself as a descendant of greatness compelled me to see myself in a very positive light as well. That trip to Little Rock Central was therefore a game changer for me. Just walking into the school forced me to raise my game even higher. It served as a personal reminder for me that I must live up to the legacy of those nine courageous students.

I did not know who I really was prior to my study of African American history. Sadly, many if not most minority students do not know themselves fully either, because they don't know their history. Couple this with the fact that a large percentage of educators do not know their minority students' history either, and you have a real recipe for disaster in the classroom (Howard, 2006).

In all my years as an educator, despite all of the professional development that I and my staff received in the form of conferences, lectures, workshops, journals, and books, I always knew that, at the end of the day, my students were not going to soar until they could answer the question "Who am I?" I knew then and I continue to be convinced today that the academic problems associated with minority students have little to do with their ability to read, write, or do math. It is my contention that these children are brilliant and most highly capable, just like anyone else. I am convinced that when given the opportunity to learn in learning environments that are conducive to them having the will to strive for excellence, they will do just that. There is no uncertainty about their ability to get the job done. My concern is their foundation, their appreciation for their brilliance, their recognition of their greatness, and their will to succeed.

In my 2009 book *Motivating Black Males to Achieve in School and in Life*, I focus on black males and their struggles to answer the question "Who am I?" relative to their history and culture. I argue that until they can answer this question and thereby gain an understanding of who they are in history, the achievement gap will not be closed. Why? Because the answer to the question "Who am I?" gives students a foundation upon which to stand, enhancing their understanding of their individual and collective roles in the continuum of society. Knowing who they are in history increases the probability that students will develop a deeper sense of purpose for their lives; it gives their existence in the world greater meaning when they know about those who struggled so that they could have the opportunities that they now have. Such historical literacy is particularly important for black and Latino students, whose histories have long been marginalized, distorted, or omitted entirely from the history books (Daniel Tatum, 2007; Hale, 1982; Kuykendall, 1992).

It is difficult for a student to answer the question "Who am I?" if his teacher is not in a position to answer the related question "Do I realize who my students are?" I dare say that tens of thousands of educators across the United States do not realize who black and Latino children are historically because they, just like their students, were never adequately educated about their history (Singleton & Linton, 2006). The end result is a lack of knowledge and understanding of who these children are on both sides—neither the students nor the teachers know who the students truly are.

Realizing Who Your Students Are

Every student in your classroom has a story. Each of them has a unique story to tell. Do you know your students' stories? Their stories define who they are as individuals. By learning their stories, you learn about them. Their stories are those life experiences that have shaped them into who they are today. As their teacher, it is incumbent upon you to learn your students' stories in an effort to learn about them.

In addition to a unique individual story, every one of your students is a part of a broader collective story as well. Each of them belongs to a racial or ethnic group, the history of which also serves to define each student. I have written extensively about this phenomenon as it relates to black students, who have a long and glorious story that must be told, studied, and learned by everyone in the United States. Unfortunately, this story has not been adequately told, studied, or learned. As a result, the answer to the question "Do I realize who my students are?" is all too often, essentially, "No."

It is imperative that you familiarize yourself with who your students are historically. It is a must that you learn their collective stories, which can clarify the reasons for the life challenges that so many minority students face on a daily basis. When students are disconnected from who they are historically, they risk gravitating to anyone who looks like them, regardless of how destructive their behaviors may be, simply because they are offered no alternative role models who share their race or ethnicity. In order to alleviate this challenge, you must learn your students' stories and teach the stories to them.

Ensuring That Students Know Who They Are

When I look at achievement levels of black and Latino students across the country, coupled with the willingness of far too many to accept mediocrity and failure for themselves, it becomes brutally obvious to me that far too many of them are simply disconnected from their past. But the students cannot be blamed for this: If students are not exposed, we cannot blame them for not knowing their stories. How can we expect someone to conceptualize something that he doesn't know exists? He must be given the information; he must be told.

Imagine if you wake up one morning, look into your mirror, and do not recognize who is looking back at you. You look around the room and don't recognize anything about it, either; when you see your family members, they look like strangers to you. You have amnesia—a total loss of memory. Historically and culturally speaking, this is the reality of too many minority students. They do not recognize who that is looking back at them in their mirrors. They have cultural amnesia—a total loss of historical and cultural memory.

The Importance of Students Learning Their Story

From the beginning of the school year to the end, the pressure on teachers to produce is enormous. Teachers teach in a world where state standardized assessment scores are the number-one priority. In most cases, this means that there is an intense focus on math, reading, and writing achievement in particular. In addition to normal school hours, students may be required to come in an hour early, stay an hour late, or spend a few hours on a Saturday morning receiving additional help in these three core subjects.

Having students spend countless hours preparing for tests in an effort to close the achievement gap implies that what students need is more time on task. I do not believe that they do; I believe they simply require a level playing field. Because these students are disconnected from their stories, they lack purpose for learning. When your students become aware of the power of their past, they will have a far greater understanding and appreciation for the power within themselves to accomplish whatever they set their sights on.

Ensuring That Students Understand the Importance of Learning Their Story

> When you control a man's thinking you do not have to worry about his actions. You do not have to tell him not to stand here or go yonder. He will find his "proper place" and will stay in it. You do not need to send him to the back door. He will go without being told. In fact, if there is no back door, he will cut one for his special benefit. His education makes it necessary.

The above quote, which I recite in all my presentations, is from Carter G. Woodson's 1933 classic *The Mis-Education of the Negro*. Far too many minority students don't want to know the history of their people because they see "history" as yet another difficult and boring subject to learn. In a sense, their thinking is controlled by what they have or haven't been exposed to. When teachers complain to me that their students seem not to want to know their history, I say to them, of course they don't—for the reasons Carter G. Woodson elucidates in his famous quote.

I have been lucky enough in my career to come across young people who are actually passionate about learning their history. They feel that it belongs to them and they have a right to learn it. In fact, many of them begin to resent their schools and districts for not teaching their history fully. When these students looked at the crime, violence, gangs, and drugs in their communities, it became clear to them that such scourges were the culmination of a lack of knowledge among a people of their shared history. They understood the layers of damage created, but also understood the importance of exposing their peers to their story.

An Educator's Responsibility to Teach Students Their Story

Social studies and history teachers understand the importance of teaching students their story, but what about the other subject areas? What about the math teacher, or the science teacher? Do these teachers have a responsibility to teach their students their story as well? Yes, indeed.

So many of the underprivileged minority students I've come across have given up hope because they felt they could never meet the challenges they were confronted with, resolving instead to living a lifestyle centered on day-to-day survival. Many of these students have shared with me that they felt they couldn't learn in school because their fellow students were out of control; some even told me that their peers pressured them to underperform, because in their minds, to be smart is to be uncool and thereby unacceptable. Students who stand out and exhibit their brilliance can end up ridiculed, harassed, isolated, and even physically harmed. Compounding the matter for children of color is the fact that so many go home to fatherless households, which often leads to anger issues. It is no wonder, then, that so many brilliant and highly capable students give up, lose hope, or short-change themselves before reaching their senior year in high school.

Despite these realities, you have the power to make the students in your classroom soar. You are a life-changer and a life-builder; you have the tools and the resources to make your students believe they can fly. One of those tools is the ability to teach your students the story of who they are. No matter what challenges your students may be grappling with today, there are people who look just like them who grew up with similar (if not worse) challenges, defied the odds, and went on to do extraordinary things with their lives. They were dealt the same hand as your students, but for whatever the reasons, they pressed on. They didn't give up; they didn't quit; they weren't willing to accept defeat. They were determined to achieve success and had the will to get the job done. These people *are* your students' story—if you expose your students to their extraordinary histories, they will be able to relate to and identify with them.

It's not necessary to teach your students their story in history class. The lives of great minority scientists or inventors might be better taught in science class, for example, just as the lives of great minority mathematicians or engineers may be taught in math class, or the lives of writers or educators in English class. I still recall my initial reaction of intrigue when I first read about the following prominent black inventors:

- Lewis Latimer—invented the electric lamp and the carbon filament for lightbulbs, wrote the first book on electric lighting, designed blueprints for the first telephone
- Granville T. Woods—invented the third rail of the electric railway system, an induction telegraph system for trains, and the automatic air brake
- Jan Matzeliger—invented the automatic shoe lasting machine for attaching soles to shoes

- Norbert Rillieux—invented the evaporating pan for refining sugar
- Frederick M. Jones—invented a refrigeration unit for trucks and trains, a ticket dispensing machine, and a portable X-ray machine
- Elijah McCoy—invented an automatic lubrication system for machines
- Garrett A. Morgan—invented the automatic traffic signal and gas mask

These inventors are just a small part of the story, but reading about them early on inspired me to want to do more. I had no idea that such scientific ingenuity was a part of my historical past. Your students will be equally inspired.

The context in which you introduce your students to their story is very important. For example, whenever I speak to an audience, before I utter the first word, I always analyze my audience and try tailoring my message to them. As a presenter, the worst thing I can do is deliver a message that has no relevance to my audience. The same holds true in the classroom: You must consider who your students are and ensure that your lessons are culturally relevant, responsive, and sensitive to all of them.

Students' Responsibility to Learn Their Story

During the time of slavery in the United States, many tactics were used to ensure that slaves remained captive *ad infinitum*. The most potent tactic was to deny slaves the right to read and write, thereby depriving them of the knowledge of who they were historically. The slave owners understood clearly that if their slaves knew how to read and write or knew their historical past, it would be difficult to contain them for long. (The abolitionist and ex-slave Frederick Douglass is a perfect example: Once he learned to read and write at a young age, he was of no further use to the slavery system and he eventually escaped.) To this day, much of the information about African and African American history has never been properly restored in the classroom, so historical ignorance persists among too many black students. This is especially unfortunate because the history of African achievements prior to slavery can be felt in a wide variety of disciplines, including science and technology, engineering and architecture, astrology and astronomy, and mathematics. If we are to close the attitude gap (and, by extension, the achievement gap), we must not only expose our students to their history in the classroom but ensure that they feel a sense of responsibility for learning their history as well.

Ensuring That Lessons Take Students' Story into Consideration

I recently conducted a professional development workshop at a school on the first teacher workday following summer break. Prior to my presentation, the teachers all met their fourth principal in five years for the first time. As the new principal spoke, I listened, but I also studied the teachers' reactions. I looked into their eyes, at their body language, and at their facial expressions. I could only imagine what their thoughts were, given the number of principals they had seen over the years.

Then it was my turn to speak. Instead of launching into my normal opening, I told the teachers to exhale and take about five minutes to talk with one another and process what they had just heard from their new principal. When the five minutes were up and I transitioned into my topic, I knew I needed to take into account the teachers' current situation throughout the day. I wanted to make sure that I met the teachers' specific needs, including those related to the reality of a new principal. I had to take "their story" into consideration for maximum effectiveness.

When I was a classroom teacher, I taught in a city that was 98 percent black. I knew that a generic approach to reaching my students was not going to be enough. I needed my lessons to speak directly to who my students were historically and culturally. For example, in mathematics, I needed to juxtapose the lessons I was teaching with the historical origins of the concepts, many of which originated in Africa. At the same time, I needed to make the math meaningful and relevant to students' lives in and outside of school. In other words, I had to relate my lessons both to "their story" and to their daily lives.

The same held true across subject areas. In language arts, for example, I wanted my students to be fully aware of the many great black writers in U.S. history, so I exposed them to such authors as James Baldwin, Gwendolyn Brooks, Countee Cullen, Paul Lawrence Dunbar, Ralph Ellison, and Langston Hughes (among many others). Not only did I want my students to know of the existence of these black writers, but I also wanted them to be aware of the stories they were telling in their books—stories which, taken as a whole, were essentially the story of my students. Of course, it's in social studies or history class where, theoretically, the story can be told from start to finish.

When planning lessons, you must take who your students are into consideration. You must infuse their story into your lessons. As I noted previously, your lessons must be culturally relevant, responsive, and sensitive for all of your learners. This doesn't mean squeezing history lessons into every subject, but it does mean being aware of your students' racial, ethnic, or cultural backgrounds and tailoring your instruction accordingly.

Helping Students Identify with and Relate to What You Teach

Do your students relate to and identify with what you teach? Do they perceive it as being relevant to their lives? Can they see where what you teach is useful to their lives? Too many underprivileged students do poorly in school because they do not perceive the information they're taught to be useful. To combat this, you must ensure that your students see themselves at the heart of the lessons that you teach. When I was a classroom teacher, I often tweaked my lessons to make them relevant for my students. I wanted them to see themselves at the heart of what I was teaching across all subject areas. You must do the same.

How Knowing "Their Story" Affects the Way Students See Themselves

Just before writing this, I was listening to a discussion of urban crime on talk radio. Apparently in this instance, 9- and 10-year-old inner-city boys had been engaging in armed carjackings and break-ins. Two dynamics are at play here: Those exploiting these children, and the children themselves. In both cases, we are looking at individuals who simply do not understand their societal roles relative to their place in the continuum of history. In large part because they do not see themselves as heirs to a great legacy, they ended up engaging in criminal behaviors.

One of your primary responsibilities is to affect the way your students see themselves. They must see themselves as the continuation of a long lineage of historical greatness and accomplishment and as highly capable of achieving what-ever challenges you present in your classroom. An absence of historical foundation leaves them in the dark, unaware of who they are in the collective sense and, therefore, of what their roles and responsibilities are as individuals. When they are exposed to their history, they gain a much broader sense of who they are and what they are capable of achieving, which has the added benefit of decreasing the likelihood that they will engage in reprehensible behaviors outside of school.

How Knowing "Their Story" Affects the Way You See Your Students

Knowing their story *must* affect the way you see your students. You must see all your students as winners, as superstars, as students who can and will achieve at the highest levels. I regularly meet teachers all over the United States who simply do not know the history of their students (particularly those who are black or of Latino descent). These teachers only know what they have been exposed to—which, sadly, tends to include media depictions that too often are negative, superficial, or stereotypical. Learning about the contributions and struggles of your students' ancestors and seeing them as descendants of such greatness is bound to affect your view of them. Seeing your students as highly capable superstars is crucial, but seeing them as part of a historical continuum is indispensable.

CONCLUSION

Over the past 20 years, I have been blessed to receive over 100 educational, professional, and community awards. Each award is special and I treasure them all. Recently, however, I received an award that I rank a little higher than all of the others, particularly in the context of this book. My alma mater—Kean University in Union, New Jersey—recently awarded me its Distinguished Alumni Award. When I received the letter advising me that I was going to receive this award, I was truly elated; I felt as though it was the culmination of my work in education at this juncture of my mission.

When I entered Kean University back in 1984, I had spent the previous five years following high school doing virtually nothing. My high school years represented the worst years of my life: I was an absolutely horrible student because my attitude toward school and life was beyond poor. Upon entering Kean University, through a series of circumstances that included my independent study of African American history (and, therefore, the story of myself), I became a changed man. I had a new attitude for success; I was hungry, focused, and driven. I was eager to be the best young man that I could be, and I now had the right attitude to make it happen.

Since my years at Kean University, I have not deviated from my very narrow path and singular purpose: to motivate, educate, and empower students, and to maintain a passion for getting it done. In order to experience the level of success I have experienced over the years, my attitude was key: The work is not easy by any stretch of the imagination, but it is extremely rewarding emotionally, and it is my attitude that has enabled me to stay the course and continue to affect the lives of thousands.

When I talk about my own journey, I am actually talking about *your students*—particularly those who are at risk of failing, as I was when I was younger. Although your students' challenges may be great today, their successes will be enormous tomorrow if you remain relentless about closing the attitude gap in your classroom. If your students' attitude is focused on success, then success is theirs for the taking.

Since writing the first words of this book back in July of 2012, I have literally spoken to thousands of children at the elementary, middle, and high school levels. Many of these children are considered to be at risk of failing—not because they aren't brilliant, but because the circumstances of their lives have led us to think of them that way. Although we as educators cannot necessarily change students' immediate circumstances outside of school, we can definitely change their attitudes toward themselves, their education, and the prospects for their futures—and if this book can affect just one student's life by reaching a teacher or school leader, then I can say that my writing was not in vain.

BIBLIOGRAPHY

Alonso, G., Anderson, N. S., Su, C., & Theoharis, J. (2009). *Our schools suck: Students talk back to a segregated nation on the failures of urban education.* New York: New York University Press.

Bailey, B. (2011). *Creating the school family: Bully-proofing classrooms through emotional intelligence.* Oviedo, FL: Loving Guidance, Inc.

Barth, R. S. (1990). *Improving schools from within.* San Francisco: Jossey-Bass.

Brendtro, L. K., Brokenleg, M., & Van Bockern, S. (1990). *Reclaiming youth at risk: Our hope for the future.* Bloomington, IN: Solution Tree Press.

Brooks, J. S. (2012). *Black school/white culture: Racism and educational (mis)leadership.* New York: Teachers College Press.

Brucato, J. M. (2005). *Creating a learning environment: An educational leader's guide to managing school culture.* Lanham, MD: Scarecrow Education.

Capper, A. C., & Frattura, E. M. (2009). *Meeting the needs of students of all abilities: How leaders go beyond inclusion.* Thousand Oaks, CA: Corwin Press.

Curwin, R. L. (2010). *Meeting students where they live: Motivation in urban schools.* Alexandria, VA: ASCD.

Cushman, K. (2003). *Fires in the bathroom: Advice for teachers from high school students.* New York: The New Press.

Daniel Tatum, T. (2007) *Can we talk about race? And other conversations in an era of school resegregation.* Boston, MA: Beacon Press.

Darling-Hammond. L. (2010). *The flat world and education.* New York: Teachers College Press.

Deal, T. E., & Peterson, K. D. (1999). *Shaping school culture: The heart of leadership.* San Francisco: Jossey-Bass.

Delpit, L. (2006). *Other people's children: Cultural conflict in the classroom.* New York: The New Press.

Delpit, L. (2012). *"Multiplication is for white people": Raising expectations for other people's children.* New York: The New Press.

Delpit, L., & Kilgour Dowdy, J. (2002). *The skin that we speak: Thoughts on language and culture in the classroom.* New York: The New Press.

Edwards, J. (2010). *Inviting students to learn: 100 tips for talking effectively with your students.* Alexandria, VA: ASCD.

Elbot, C. F., & Fulton, D. (2008). *Building an intentional school culture: Excellence in academics and character.* Thousand Oaks, CA: Corwin Press.

Eller, J. F., & Eller, S. (2009). *Creative strategies to transform school culture.* Thousand Oaks, CA: Corwin Press/NASSP.

Fay, J., & Cline, F. W. (2000). *The pearls of love and logic for parents and teachers.* Golden, CO: Love and Logic Institute, Inc.

Fay, J., & Funk, D. (1995*). Teaching with love and logic: Taking control of the classroom.* Golden, CO: Love and Logic Institute, Inc.

Fisher, D., Frey, N., & Pumpian, I. (2012). *How to create a culture of achievement in your school and classroom.* Alexandria, VA: ASCD.

Foster, M. (1997) *Black teachers on teaching.* New York: The New Press.

Gay, G. (2000). *Culturally responsive teaching: Theory, research and practice.* New York: Teachers College Press.

Hale, J. (1982). *Black children: Their roots, culture and learning styles.* Baltimore: Johns Hopkins University Press.

Hart, S., & Kindle Hodson, V. (2004). *The compassionate classroom: Relationship-based teaching and learning.* Encinitas, CA: Puddle Dancer Press.

Howard, G. (2006). *We can't teach what we don't know.* New York: Teachers College Press.

Howard, T. C. (2010). *Why race and culture matters in schools: Closing the achievement gap in America's classrooms.* New York: Teachers College Press.

Jackson, R. (2009). *Never work harder than your students & other principles of great teaching.* Alexandria, VA: ASCD.

Jackson, R. R. (2011). *How to motivate reluctant learners.* Alexandria, VA: ASCD; Washington, DC: Mindsteps.

Jensen, E. (2009). *Teaching with poverty in mind: What being poor does to kids' brains and what schools can do about it.* Alexandria, VA: ASCD.

Kafele, B. (2004). *A handbook for teachers of African American children.* Jersey City, NJ: Baruti Publishing.

Kafele, B. (2009). *Motivating black males to achieve in school and in life.* Alexandria, VA: ASCD.

Kohn, A. (2006). *Beyond discipline: From compliance to community.* Alexandria, VA: ASCD.

Kruse, S. D., & Seashore Louis, K. (2009). *Building strong school cultures: A guide to leading change.* Thousand Oaks, CA: Corwin Press/Leadership for Learning.

Kuykendall, C. (1992) *From rage to hope: Strategies for reclaiming black and Hispanic students.* Bloomington, IN: National Educational Service.

Ladson-Billings, G. (1994). *The Dreamkeepers: Successful teachers of African American children.* San Francisco: Jossey-Bass.

Lemov, D. (2010). *Teach like a champion: 49 techniques that put students on the path to college.* San Francisco: Jossey-Bass.

Mackenzie, R. J., & Stanzione, L. (2010). *Setting limits in the classroom.* New York: Three Rivers Press.

Mendler, A. N. (2001). *Connecting with students.* Alexandria, VA: ASCD.

Mendler, A. N. (2012). *When teaching gets tough: Smart ways to reclaim your game.* Alexandria, VA: ASCD.

Nelson, J., Lott, L., & Glenn, H. S. (2000). *Positive discipline in the classroom.* New York: Three Rivers Press.

Olson, K. (2009). *Wounded by school: Recapturing the joy in learning and standing up to old school culture.* New York: Teachers College Press.

Parrett, W. H., & Budge, K. M. (2012). *Turning high-poverty schools into high-performing schools.* Alexandria, VA: ASCD.

Preble, B., & Gordon, R. (2011). *Transforming school climate and learning: Beyond bullying and compliance.* Thousand Oaks, CA: Corwin Press.

Rajagopal, K. (2011). *Create success: Unlocking the potential of urban students.* Alexandria, VA: ASCD.

Reeves, D. B. (2004). *Accountability for learning: How teachers and school leaders can take charge.* Alexandria, VA: ASCD.

Ridnouer, K. (2006). *Managing your classroom with heart: A guide to nurturing adolescent learners.* Alexandria, VA: ASCD.

Rodriguez, E. R. (2007). *What is it about me you can't teach?* Thousand Oaks, CA: Corwin Press.

Schafft, K. A., & Youngblood Jackson, A. (2010). *Rural education for the twenty-first century.* University Park: The Pennsylvania State University Press.

Schott Foundation for Public Education. (2008). *Given half a chance: The Schott 50-state report on public education and black males.* Cambridge, MA: Author.

Singleton, G. E., & Linton, C. W. (2006). *Courageous conversations about race.* Thousand Oaks, CA: Corwin Press.

Sprick, R. S. (2006). *Discipline in the secondary classroom: A positive approach to behavior management.* San Francisco, CA: Jossey-Bass.

Sterrett, W. (2011). *Insights into action: Successful school leaders share what works.* Alexandria, VA: ASCD.

Stutzman Amstutz, L., & Mullet, J. H. (2005). *The little book of restorative discipline for schools: Teaching responsibility; creating caring climates.* Intercourse, PA: Good Books.

Sullo, B. (2007). *Activating the desire to learn.* Alexandria, VA: ASCD.

Sullo, B. (2009). *The motivated student: Unlocking the enthusiasm for learning.* Alexandria, VA: ASCD.

Tatum, A. W. (2009). *Reading for their life: Building the textual lineages of African American adolescent males.* Portsmouth, NH: Heinemann.

Weiner, L. (2006). *Urban teaching: The essentials.* New York: Teachers College Press.

Wessler, S. L. (2003). *The respectful school: How educators and students can conquer hate and harassment.* Alexandria, VA: ASCD.

Wong, H. K., & Wong, R. T. (2009). *The first days of school: How to be an effective teacher.* Mountain View, CA: Harry K. Wong Publications, Inc.

Zoul, J. (2010). *Building school culture one week at a time.* Larchmont, NY: Eye on Education.

ABOUT THE
AUTHOR

Who Is Baruti K. Kafele?

Baruti K. Kafele, affectionately known as "Principal Kafele," excelled as an urban public school educator in New Jersey for more than 20 years. As an elementary school teacher in East Orange, he was selected as the East Orange School District and Essex County Public Schools Teacher of the Year. As a middle and high school principal, he led the transformation of four different schools, including Newark Tech High School, which went from a low-performing school in need of improvement to being recognized by *U.S. News and World Report* three times as one of the best high schools in the United States.

Principal Kafele is currently a highly sought-after education speaker and consultant. He travels extensively throughout the United States and abroad, spreading his empowering message of *attitude transformation*. A versatile and passionate speaker, he regularly conducts conference keynote addresses; professional development workshops for educators; parental engagement seminars; and hard-hitting, no-nonsense student empowerment assemblies.

Principal Kafele earned his bachelor's degree in management science/marketing from Kean University, where he graduated *summa cum laude,* and his master's degree in educational administration from New Jersey City University. He is the author of five books—including his national best-seller, *Motivating Black Males to Achieve in School and in Life* (ASCD, 2009)—and has received more that 100 educational, professional, and community awards, including the Kean University Distinguished Alumni Award (2013), the New Jersey Education Association Award of Excellence (2011), and the Milken National Educator Award (2009). In 1998, a proclamation from the City of Dickinson, Texas, declared February 8, 1998, to be Baruti K. Kafele Day.